SIR WALTER SCOTT
LECTURES

SIR WALTER SCOTT

STATUE IN THE LAIGH PARLIAMENT HALL
NATIONAL LIBRARY OF SCOTLAND

From a woodcut by Miss Joan Hassall
Reproduced by permission of the Edinburgh Bibliographical Society

SIR HERBERT GRIERSON ✦ EDWIN MUIR
G. M. YOUNG ✦ S. C. ROBERTS

SIR WALTER SCOTT LECTURES

1940–1948

[by] Edinburgh. University

With an Introduction by
PROFESSOR W. L. RENWICK

EDINBURGH
AT THE UNIVERSITY PRESS
1950

COPYRIGHT

PRINTED IN GREAT BRITAIN
BY R. & R. CLARK, LTD, EDINBURGH

CONTENTS

	PAGE
Introduction	vii

1940

Sir Herbert Grierson   1
    I. THE MAN AND THE POET
    II. HISTORY AND THE NOVEL

1944

Edwin Muir   53
    I. WALTER SCOTT: THE MAN
    II. WALTER SCOTT: THE WRITER

1946

G. M. Young   79
    SCOTT AND THE HISTORIANS

1948

S. C. Roberts   109
    I. THE MAKING OF A NOVELIST
    II. THE FATE OF A NOVELIST

Index   167

INTRODUCTION

THIS volume contains the Sir Walter Scott Memorial Lectures delivered in the University of Edinburgh by the first four lecturers on that foundation.

They are concerned, as it happens, with Scott the historian and Scott the novelist; and it becomes increasingly clear that the two were one. His acquaintance Henry Cockburn says of *The Lay of the Last Minstrel*: " The subject . . . was, for the period, singularly happy. It recalled scenes and times and characters so near as almost to linger in the memory of the old, and yet so remote that their revival, under poetical embellishment, imparted the double pleasure of invention and of history." He was born at the right time and in the right place. He knew Liddesdale before it had roads, still self-sufficing as it had been for centuries. He heard the story of the '45 from men who had been out with their clans and had lived through the violent transition from Celtic tribalism to something like modern parliamentary government. There has been nothing like it since, in these islands. So he had touch with modes of life that stretched back into remote ages, and his multifarious enquiries into history, tradition, superstition, pageantry, literature and song, made more concrete by the multifarious collection of relics that we can still see in Abbotsford, gave him touch with men who chanced to have died before he was born, whose general memory he tried to keep alive with humane piety, and whose ways and doings gave him store of imagery which he used joyfully to express his brave sense of life and his delight in life.

He was not in bondage to the past, but used his knowledge freely. The imagined date of *The Lay of the Last Minstrel* is about 1555; but the old monk of Melrose was a disciple of Michael Scott, who died about 1285; one of the Scottish chiefs is Walter Scott of Harden, who was not more than five years old in 1555, and the English chief is Lord William Howard, who was not born till 1565. This was not carelessness, for of all history this was the history Walter Scott knew. He was choosing his symbols: the dead Buccleuch, killed in 1552, the victim of the deadly feud that was the curse of the Border and one premise of his romantic tale; Auld Wat of Harden, *par excellence* the competent leader of border horse; Belted Will Howard, the ideal courteous, placable English aristocrat; and so on. All these are historically true, separately. Scott brings each forward in the guise he commonly presents in tradition, to serve his place in a whole which is, frankly and deliberately, romantic. The story is a free invention; the spirit of it is true—true as music is true, proving nothing and demonstrating nothing.

His independence of dead values is obvious in *The Monastery*. He collected and revered the ballads and traditions of his beloved Border, and all that kept alive the memory of the old rough times of rugging and riving. He prided himself on his descent from various hard-bitten moss-trooping lairds who balanced their budgets by the light of the Michaelmas moon. But in this novel of the heyday of the moss-troopers he had to prove or demonstrate, or at least suggest, the balance of right and wrong, good and evil. And his picture of the Border lord is thoroughly adverse. Johnnie Armstrong is a figure of romantic admiration only in the reminiscences of a blethering old woman; Christie of Clinthill is a cruel, greedy, second-rate ruffian with courage for his only virtue, an anachronism, an unimportant piece of flotsam in a world intent on graver issues. It is a kind of disillusion, if you like the word; but it is the right kind of disillusion, that is not catastrophic and grows out of common sense. With all his love of an exciting and picturesque past, Scott realised all too clearly how salutary was the work of the kings who hanged Johnnie Armstrong at his own gate and made the key keep the castle and the rush-bush keep the cow. He had no more desire to return to moss-trooping than to the ox-plough and the runrig system of agriculture. The hill was the more interesting that it had been the scene of battle and foray, but it was better that the sheep should graze in peace, that the shepherd should walk his round unarmed, sure to find the thatch still on his cottage when he came home at nightfall.

For the thing that vivified past and present alike was the perennial spring of human interest that underlay his antiquarian piety and his daily conversation. If ever a man lived in good-will among his neighbours, it was Sir Walter; his lively and kindly good-will embraced past generations within his neighbourhood and also kept him from undervaluing the present. The old days were good to talk about and sing about, a glorious background for the present. He delighted in their beauty and strenuousness, believed in the virtues of head and heart they bred and displayed, but he knew they had to go—not merely for reasons of economics or hygiene or police, but because that is the law of life. Yet past and present are one. The present is not more real than the past, nor the past more valid than the present, and there is no hiatus between them.

So it is proper that a statue of Sir Walter should stand where our frontispiece shows it: among the books and manuscripts the Faculty of Advocates gave to form the Scottish National Library—a statue which is, according to old Parliament House tradition, the most living likeness of the man. It is proper also that another should sit facing the crowds in Princes Street. For past and present are but terms for fragments in the unity of life; and it was he, the poet, historian, and novelist, that taught us the lesson.

W. L. RENWICK

SIR HERBERT GRIERSON
1940

Reprinted from
The University of Edinburgh Journal 1940–41
Vol. XI, Nos. 1 and 2

I
THE MAN AND THE POET

A GREAT creative artist is almost necessarily a somewhat complex character. He lives at least a twofold life (and he may live more): the life of the imagination, of the aspirations and sorrows which inspire his lyrical poetry—

> We look before and after,
> And pine for what is not,—

the characters and incidents of his own creation, their individualities, and the fortune which befalls them; on the other hand, he is living his own life in the world, this world of practical realities, money to be made, responsibilities to be incurred by his relation to other persons—wife, children, friends, fellow-citizens. It is a not uninteresting study to consider how these lives invade one another: Shakespeare's plays and Shakespeare's dreams of returning to Stratford-on-Avon as a respected and influential citizen with a coat-of-arms; Scott's poems and novels and his dreams of purchasing land, building himself a noble mansion, and founding a Border family; the effect, again, of these more worldly dreams on their imaginative creations, making them apparently content with work which served its practical purpose while falling short of artistic perfection. There would then remain the question how far the imaginative work affected, on the other hand, the practical life. Nor are these all the complexities in which a life dominated by the imagination may find itself involved.

In no great writer is this complexity of life and character more obvious than in Sir Walter Scott, who lived three lives at least, keeping each as far as possible independent of the other, and two of them concealed from the public, and that despite the air of frankness, of " easy openness " which pervades all he wrote whether in verse or prose. " A winning air of candour," declares a critic of whom I shall have more to say, pervades Scott's *Life of Dryden* and the Waverley Novels " which deserves to be numbered among their chief excellencies. They urge opinions and impart knowledge in the frank, unassuming and courteous manner of a friend communicating with a friend." And this air of friendly openness was felt by everyone who knew Scott not only through his works but in person.

Yet there were depths and cross-currents underneath the open, sunny surface which Scott presented to the world : " What a strange scene," he writes in 1825, " if the surge of conversation could suddenly ebb like the tide and show us the state of people's real minds . . .

>   No eyes the rocks discover
>   Which lurk beneath the deep.

Life could not be endured were it seen in reality."

The critic whom I have mentioned, a certain

John Adolphus, was the author in 1821 of a series of letters to Richard Heber, in which he undertook to identify the author of the then anonymous Waverley Novels with the Walter Scott who had composed certain popular poems and other works. Alongside of a number of lesser points of resemblance, as that the author of both is an Edinburgh man, a lawyer, one that is fond of sport and especially of dogs, a man interested in military affairs but not a soldier, Adolphus singles out four main aspects of the work of the two authors, if they be two, qualities which had made the novels so great a source of pleasure to readers and distinguished them from the work of predecessors and contemporaries.

The author is a poet. Innumerable passages in the novels are "the writing of one who has always looked at objects with the eye of a poet, and unavoidably speaks of them as he sees them." He is also a man of good society, a gentleman; an impression, Adolphus insists, conveyed by the work of very few poets and novelists of the day. Thirdly, "All the productions . . . both of the poet and of the prose writer, recommend themselves by a native piety and goodness, not generally predominant in modern works of imagination, and which, when they do appear, are too often disfigured by eccentricity, pretension, or bad taste. In the works before us there is a constant tendency to promote the desire of excellence in ourselves, and the love of it in our neighbours, by making us think honourably of our general nature."

Lastly: " Good sense, the sure foundation of

excellence in all the arts, is another leading characteristic of these productions." A poet, a gentleman, a writer with a deep respect for religion and conduct, a man of eminently good sense—such is the impression conveyed by a study of the novels to one who had no personal acquaintance with the man. How far is it borne out by our fuller knowledge of Scott's life?

The question of the poet I will leave over for a little, as the interaction of the imagination of the poet and the good sense of the man of the world in Scott's narrative poems and novels will be my chief theme. Scott's good sense is enlarged upon by another critic, Walter Bagehot. He finds it in Scott's delineation of great political events and influential political institutions. These descriptions are not always accurate or uncoloured by his feelings: "Still, whatever period or incident we take, we shall always find in the error a great, in one or two cases perhaps an extreme, mixture of the mental element which we term common-sense." We find it again in Scott's picture of the poor in which he avoids "fancied happiness and Arcadian simplicity" on the one hand, and on the other the wretched meanness of realism such as Crabbe's, or sentimentalism as in Dickens. Scott's "poor people are never coarse and never vulgar; their lineaments have the rude traits which a life of conflict will inevitably leave on the minds and manners of those who are to lead it; their notions have the narrowness which is inseparable from a contracted experience; their knowledge is not more extended than their restricted means of attaining it would render possible. Almost alone among novelists Scott has given a thorough, minute, lifelike description of poor persons, which is at the same time genial and pleasing." Nevertheless this man, whose eminent good sense shines in all he writes and was obvious to all who met him, not least in his advice to others, permitted his imagination, his wishes, to lead him into financial schemes the sheer folly of which is undeniable, induced him to establish a printing house the profits of which he always overestimated, and persuaded him to set up for a time as publisher though he had no conception of the gulf between his own antiquarian, historical and literary interests and the taste of the general reading public. He continued throughout his life to meet current expenses by drafts upon future works, anticipation of gains to come.

That Scott was in real life the gentleman whose presence Adolphus divined in the novels is confirmed by all who knew Scott in the flesh: by Lord Cockburn, who disliked his politics; by Sydney Smith, who writes, "who in the ordinary intercourse of society is better bred . . . ?"; by Maria Edgeworth, who had moved in the best society both in London and in Paris, "Walter Scott is one of the best bred-men I ever saw, with all the exquisite politeness which he knew so well how to describe, which is of no particular school or country, but which is of all countries, the politeness which arises from good and quick sense and feeling, which seems to know by instinct the characters of others, to see what will please and put all his guests at their ease." Yet this gentleman in the best sense of the word was a keen, even a little unscrupulous, man of business in his dealings with publishers. He borrowed money from his friends without clearly indicating the risk which they were running. While accepting the confidence of those friends he concealed from them entirely the facts of his financial speculations. It is clear that this is what his son-in-law felt most acutely after the failure, and Lockhart was himself a sufferer by that failure. Even his wife's dowry had been paid by a bill, a draft on the future, so that she too became a creditor in the bankruptcy.

And what of Adolphus's intuition that the author of the novels was a religious man, that they reveal a native piety and goodness? A very difficult question, the answer to which would depend very much on the individual's own conception of a religious character. Bagehot notes as the greatest want of the novels any interest in " the searching and abstract intellect," any coherent philosophy of life; and this is in the main true. Underneath Scott's sparkling, animated picture of life lies a melancholy not unlike that of Dr. Johnson, whose *Vanity of Human Wishes* was his favourite poem. Nevertheless, I think Adolphus's impression was a just one. Scott did not love saints; as he saw them, the " unco guid." He warns James Ballantyne of all things not to marry a very religious woman, for nothing can be a greater cause of unhappiness in a family.

But Bagehot, I think, is mistaken in his description of Scott's religious feeling. "He was," Bagehot says, "a genial man of the world and had the easy faith in the kindly *Dieu des bonnes gens* which is natural to such a person; and he had also a half-poetic principle of superstition in his nature, inclining him to believe in ghosts, legends, fairies, and elves, which did not affect his daily life or possibly his superficial belief, but was nevertheless very constantly present to his fancy." I think Bagehot misapprehends, or exaggerates, both these tendencies. God for Scott was the God of his Presbyterian upbringing, a judge before whom everyone would have to render his account: "There is a God and a just God—a judgment and a future life—and all who own so much let them act according to the faith that is in them." As to the superstitions of the peasantry, they were, Scott felt, essential elements in the mind of the common people as he knew them—*that* was their reality. But the deepest religious instinct in Scott's mind was that which Adolphus indicates when he speaks of Scott "making us think honourably of our general nature." "He censures God," says Burke, "who quarrels with the imperfections of man." That is what Scott felt deeply. Such a contempt for humanity as was expressed by Swift bordered on blasphemy. "The *Voyage to the Land of the Houyhnhnms* is a composition an editor of Swift must ever consider with pain. The source of such a diatribe against human nature could only be that fierce indignation which he has described in his epitaph as so long gnawing his heart." If a respect for and love of the best elements in human nature is not a strand in religious feeling, what, one might ask, is the significance of the doctrine of the Incarnation? But Scott combined this with another strand of feeling—entire resignation to the will of God. "He has given and shall He not take away?" is a recurring expression, if at times the same thought is given a more stoical turn: "The fact is, I belong to that set of philosophers who ought to be called Nymmites after their good founder Corporal Nym and the fundamental maxim of whose school is 'things must be as they may.'" But the chief evidence is in the *Journal*. In all the records of toil and pain and loss and occasional bitterness of feeling one note is entirely absent, that with which Thomas Hardy and A. E. Housman have made us familiar—there is no arraignment of Providence, no indictment of the "President of the Immortals."

And lastly as to the poet, Adolphus's contention that the same combination of the imagination of a poet with the good sense of a man who has a firm grasp of reality is equally evident in the poems and in the novels? Scott's poetry is somewhat at a discount to-day. Whether the poetry of the first forty years of this century will be judged great poetry is a question that must be left to a succeeding generation, which can see it in better perspective, to decide. It certainly may be reckoned the most sophisticated poetry, in thought, feeling and form, which our literature has produced. Strangely enough, the three chief incursions of American influence in English poetry have all made for some consciously elaborated sophistication—Edgar Allan Poe, Walt Whitman and T. S. Eliot. Poe and Eliot might seem to stand at opposite poles from one another. What unites them in my mind is the amazing virtuosity of each. In Poe the element of thought is of the slightest, subordinated entirely to effects of suggestion and colour and music. In Eliot's poetry there is a deeper substratum of thought; but even more elaborate is the virtuosity with which the poet's reaction to the thought is elaborated. Compared with poetry of this sophisticated kind Scott's poetry has something of the charm of a clear running stream, a burn running over stones and shadowed by heathery braes and trees which, as autumn advances, take on a rich colour. It is in his lyrics that Scott is most purely a poet, but that in a way of his own. He did not achieve success in the early personal lyrics, evoked by his passion for Miss Belsches, only one of which, "The Violet," was ever printed in his lifetime. The two which were unearthed recently at Abbotsford make no great addition, though they shed an interesting light on Scott's character and his feelings at that time. It was when, under the influence of Matthew Gregory Lewis, he began not only to collect but to imitate the romantic Scottish ballads that he found himself as a poet. There was something like a kink in Scott's mind which made him most a poet, not when expressing his own feelings, but when writing as though he were someone else, some older writer of ballads,

of songs, or hymns, or fragments of old plays.
The best of his poems are not the narrative lays
of which I shall have more to say later, but the
ballads and lyrics which he scattered through
both the longer poems and the prose novels.
There is the beautiful " Rosabelle " in *The Lay
of the Last Minstrel*, at once dramatic and picturesque. In *Marmion* you have the lyrical:

> Where shall the lover rest,
>   Whom the fates sever
> From his true maiden's breast,
>   Parted for ever ?
> Where through groves deep and high
>   Sounds the far billow,
> Where early violets die
>   Under the willow,
> *Eleu loro*, etc. Soft shall be his pillow.

And there is the spirited and well-known " Loch-
invar." *The Lady of the Lake* abounds in such
songs:

> Soldier, rest ! thy warfare o'er

> He is gone on the mountain,
> He is lost to the forest . . .

> The heath this night must be my bed,

the ballad:

> Merry it is in the good greenwood,

and these are only a few.
   In *Rokeby* you have the song, " To the Moon ":

> Hail to thy cold and clouded beam,

" O, Brignall banks are wild and fair," " A
weary lot is thine, fair maid," the refrain of

which is borrowed from a song by Burns that Scott must have taken to be old and traditional:

> He gave his bridal reins a shake,
> Said " Adieu for evermore,
> My love!
> And adieu for evermore,"

and there is " Allen-a-Dale " and others.

The novels abound with similar songs and fragments of songs—songs by David Gellatley and Flora Mac-Ivor in *Waverley*, the more impressive strains of Meg Merrilies in *Guy Mannering*:

> Twist ye, twine ye! even so,
> Mingle shades of joy and woe,
> Hope and fear, and peace and strife,
> In the thread of human life;

to which add the corresponding death song:

> Wasted, weary, wherefore stay,
> Wrestling thus with earth and clay?
> From the body pass away;—
> Hark! the mass is singing.

Of the song "Jock of Hazeldean," composed about the same time (1810), only the first verse is old; the rest is Scott's. In *The Antiquary* there is the fine song on time:

> Why sit'st thou by that ruin'd hall,
> Thou aged carle so stern and grey?
> Dost thou its former pride recall,
> Or ponder how it pass'd away?

and the fragments of a ballad sung by old Elspeth. In what is perhaps the most Shakespearean scene in *The Heart of Midlothian*, the death-bed scene of poor Madge Wildfire, when she sings like Ophelia in *Hamlet*, you have in succession the song of a harvest home, a verse from a methodist hymn, two verses from some old ballad, and what is perhaps the best known of Scott's songs:

> Proud Maisie is in the wood,
>   Walking so early;
> Sweet Robin sits on the bush,
>   Singing so rarely,
>
> " Tell me, thou bonny bird,
>   When shall I marry me?"—
> " When six braw gentlemen
>   Kirkward shall carry ye."
>
> " Who makes the bridal bed,
>   Birdie, say truly?"—
> " The grey-headed sexton
>   That delves the grave duly.
>
> " The glow-worm o'er grave and stone
>   Shall light thee steady;
> The owl from the steeple sing,
>   ' Welcome, proud lady.' "

But I must not attempt to enumerate many more of the songs. I would only mention—as again, like the songs of Madge Wildfire, a proof of Scott's ability to reproduce *any* kind of song with which his experience had made him familiar— Rebecca's hymn in *Ivanhoe*, somewhat in the style of the best Scottish paraphrases:

> When Israel, of the Lord beloved,
>   Out from the land of bondage came,
> Her father's God before her moved,
>   An awful guide in smoke and flame.

> By day, along the astonish'd lands
>   The cloudy pillar glided slow;
> By night, Arabia's crimson'd sands
>   Return'd the fiery column's glow.

In the same novel is the Catholic funeral hymn:

> Dust unto dust,
> To this all must;
> The tenant hath resign'd
> The faded form
> To waste and worm—
> Corruption claims her kind.
>
> Through paths unknown
> Thy soul hath flown,
> To seek the realms of woe,
> Where fiery pain
> Shall purge the stain
> Of actions done below.
>
> In that sad place,
> By Mary's grace,
> Brief may thy dwelling be!
> Till prayers and alms,
> And holy psalms,
> Shall set the captive free.

In as late a novel as *Quentin Durward* you have the fine song

> Ah! County Guy, the hour is nigh,

and in *Woodstock*, "An Hour with Thee." These are not the kinds of poetry in vogue to-day, when poetry and music have shaken hands with one another, but if they are not the songs of a poet, I do not know what are. You will note, however, their character. There is nothing in them of the deep personal feeling in the songs of Blake, or Byron, or Shelley, no metaphysical strain as in Blake's songs or those of Browning and Yeats. Their parallels are the songs scattered through Shakespeare's plays. Even Burns in his recast of folk-songs frequently charges them with more of his personal feelings, if at other times he sophisticates them by such decorations as Percy used in his versions of the ballads. The beautiful simplicity of the old song, " Here awa, there awa, here awa Willie," is in Burns's version marred by classical tags quite out of range of a village maiden. But in other songs, as " Mary Morison " or " Ae Fond Kiss " there is a depth of feeling and range of thought which is also outside the limits of genuine folk-song. Scott's revivals of older strains, aristocratic as often as folk-song, are in a purer style.

And what of the narrative poems? These have become so hackneyed by use in schools that it is difficult now to do them justice; but I wish to point out what exactly Scott was trying to do. It was, he tells us, from a ballad that *The Lay of the Last Minstrel* was developed. But Scott had, during these years, been helping his friend George Ellis in the printing of long extracts, with connecting links in prose, from many of the Middle English lays of the thirteenth to the fifteenth century, and these were doubtless in his mind when he composed his first lay. But it was from Coleridge's *Christabel* that he derived the freer, accentual, more ballad-like measure which he manages, not very happily, in *The Lay*. The important thing, however, to notice is that this lay was not intended to be a poem of the purely romantic, fairy-like character of the old Middle English lays. Scott did not attempt to do what William Morris was to do later. While busy on *The Lady of the Lake*, Scott complained in a letter of the want of the element of reality in all " modern epics," the want of everyday characters and incidents. His poems were clearly to be more akin to epic than to romance, for the difference which, since the Renaissance, had been recognised as distinguishing mediaeval romance from classical epic was that the latter dealt with an historical event, or so it was assumed. Homer's poems were, for the Greeks, the account of a historical war, and Vergil's *Æneid* was the history of the foundation of Rome. Milton accordingly rejected his first choice, the story of King Arthur, when he discovered that the history was fictitious. Scott was not, of course, aiming at anything so majestic as these poems, but his stories were to be given a definite local setting and a definite historical period. Two of them, indeed, *Marmion* and *The Lord of the Isles*, centre around great and critical events in Scottish history, Flodden and Bannockburn, and for that very reason are, taken as wholes, perhaps the least successful, though there are excellent passages in both. The greatness of the historical issues is out of proportion to the slightness of the central love story. *The Lay of the Last Minstrel* and *The Lady of the Lake* are, to my mind, more successful just because they are more purely romantic, though each of them has a sufficiently definite historical setting, —a border raid, a punitive expedition to the Highlands, both of them events of a kind that did frequently occur. *The Lady of the Lake* is the best sustained throughout because everything in it is romantic—scenery, characters, and incidents.

Not pure romance, therefore, but the romance of history and locality, was Scott's aim even in these poems, the precursors of his later prose novels. Hence, not only the story purposes to be of an event happening at a definite period, but other features of the poem have the same suggestion of truth and actuality. Consider his use of proper names. Scott quite definitely put his country on the map for readers abroad and at home. The names of hills and lakes and streams and moorland come warm from his heart. When Washington Irving visited him in the early days of Abbotsford, and was surprised at the nakedness of the country, Scott told him " if I did not see the heather at least once a year, I *think I should die.*" That expresses the spirit of the descriptions in the poems:

> Early they took Dun-Edin's road,
> And I could trace each step they trode:
> Hill, brook, nor dell, nor rook, nor stone
> Lies on the path to me unknown.
> Much might it boast of storied lore;
> But, passing such digression o'er,
> Suffice it that the route was laid
> Across the furzy hills of Braid.
> They pass'd the glen and scanty rill,
> And climb'd the opposing bank, until
> They gain'd the top of Blackford Hill.

SIR HERBERT GRIERSON

Blackford! on whose uncultured breast,
Among the broom, and thorn, and whin,
A truant-boy, I sought the nest,
Or listed, as I lay at rest,
While rose, on breezes thin,
The murmur of the city crowd,
And, from his steeple jangling loud,
Saint Giles's mingling din . . .

. . . . . .

Still on the spot Lord Marmion stay'd,
For fairer scene he ne'er survey'd.
When sated with the martial show
That peopled all the plain below,
The wandering eye could o'er it go,
And mark the distant city glow
With gloomy splendour red;
For on the smoke-wreaths, huge and slow,
That round her sable turrets flow,
The morning beams were shed,
And ting'd them with a lustre proud,
Like that which streaks a thunder-cloud.
Such dusky grandeur clothed the height,
Where the huge Castle holds its state,
And all the steep slope down,
Whose ridgy back heaves to the sky,
Piled deep and massy, close and high,
Mine own romantic town!
But northward far, with purer blaze,
On Ochil mountains fell the rays,
And as each heathy top they kissed,
It gleam'd a purple amethyst.
Yonder the shores of Fife you saw;
Here Preston-Bay and Berwick-Law:
And, broad between them rolled,
The gallant Frith the eye might note,
Whose islands on its bosom float,
Like emeralds chased in gold.

> Fitz-Eustace' heart felt closely pent;
> As if to give his rapture vent,
> The spur he to his charger lent,
> And raised his bridle hand,
> And, making demi-volte in air,
> Cried, " Where's the coward that would
>   not dare
> To fight for such a land ! "
> The Lindesay smiled his joy to see;
> Nor Marmion's frown repress'd his glee.

There had been nothing like these vivid details, this concreteness, in eighteenth-century landscape poetry, and certainly none in Scottish poetry. Thomson's winter scenes are obviously Scottish, but he mentions individual names only when he ventures out to foreign and distant lands. Of Scottish localities there is, if I remember it right, only one striking mention in *The Seasons*:

> Or where the Northern Ocean in vast whirls
> Boils round the naked, melancholy isles
> Of farthest Thule, or the Atlantic surge
> Pours in among the stormy Hebrides.

Even so he has to call Shetland by the classical name Thule. Cowper, indeed, delights in detail, but his are purely personal details. There is no such blend in his pictures of natural features with associations both personal and historical. Ossian had supplied and repeated certain aspects of Highland scenery—bare moor and stones and curling mists, poems such as " Albania " and " The Clyde " had dilated upon Scottish scenery somewhat in the manner of *The Seasons*, but with an eye quite as much to utilitarian as to picturesque features. It was Scott who made our localities romantic to all readers of poetry.

The same feeling which filled his poems with the proper names of hills and streams and lakes gave its character also to his descriptions of nature. Scott is no Wordsworth describing and interpreting the reactions of the spirit of man to the influence of external nature. He has not, as Adolphus notes, the gift of suggesting, as some poets can, by a few details far more than meets the eye, because they communicate an emotional impression which of itself helps to evoke the completer picture; as when Æschylus speaks of the " innumerable laughter " of the sea, or Shakespeare writes

> Now . . .
> . . . creeping murmur and the pouring dark
> Fills the wide vessel of the universe,

or Milton,

> The sounds and seas with all their finny drove
> Now to the moon in wavering morrice move,

or describes the battle of the angels in heaven when the war

> . . . soaring on main wing
> Tormented all the air;

or Keats describes how

> . . . upon a tranced night
> Those green-robed senators of mighty woods,
> Tall oaks, branch-charmed by the earnest stars
> Dream and so dream all night without a stir.

In such lines it is the emotion evoked by the words " laughter," " morrice," " tormented," "tranced," that quickens the imagination to fill up the picture.

The closest parallel to Scott's descriptions are those of Crabbe, with their enumeration and particular description of flowers, and trees, and mosses, and sea-weeds:

> Lo! where the heath, with withering brake grown o'er,
> Lends the light turf that warms the neighbouring poor;
> From thence a length of burning sand appears,
> Where the thin harvest waves its wither'd ears;
> Rank weeds, that every art and care defy,
> Reign o'er the land, and rob the blighted rye;
> There thistles stretch their prickly arms afar,
> And to the ragged infant threaten war.

with which compare:

> Oft in my mind such thoughts awake,
> By lone Saint Mary's silent lake;
> Thou know'st it well,—nor fen, nor sedge,
> Pollute the pure lake's crystal edge;
> Abrupt and sheer, the mountains sink
> At once upon the level brink;
> And just a trace of silver sand
> Marks where the water meets the land.
> Far in the mirror, bright and blue,
> Each hill's huge outline you may view;
> Shaggy with heath, but lonely bare,
> Nor tree, nor bush, nor brake, is there,
> Save where, of land, yon slender line
> Bears thwart the lake the scatter'd pine.

Compared with Crabbe's, Scott's descriptions are in general more stirring and passionate, less contemplative. Enthusiasm perhaps, rather than passion in a deeper sense of the word, is the dominant mood in the pieces in which he weaves together his love of nature and his love of definite localities, their associations for himself and for the lover of Scottish history:

> but still,
> When summer smiled on sweet Bowhill,
> And July's eve, with balmy breath,
> Waved the blue-bells on Newark heath;
> When throstles sung in Harehead-shaw,
> And corn was green on Carterhaugh,
> And flourish'd, broad, Blackandro's oak,
> The aged Harper's soul awoke!

or in a different key but with the same objectivity:

> Harold was born where restless seas
> Howl round the storm-swept Orcades;
> Where erst St. Clairs held princely sway
> O'er isle and islet, strait and bay;—
> Still nods their palace to its fall,
> Thy pride and sorrow, fair Kirkwall!—
> Thence oft he mark'd fierce Pentland rave,
> As if grim Odin rode her wave;
> And watch'd, the whilst with visage pale,
> And throbbing heart, the struggling sail;
> For all of wonderful and wild
> Had rapture for the lonely child.

Compared with Scott's, Crabbe's descriptions have a little more of the scientific observer, and in places a deeper vein of feeling, notably in the description of the scene in the convict's dream of the night before his death:

> They feel the calm delight, and thus proceed
> Through the green lane, then linger in the mead,
> Stray o'er the heath in all its purple bloom,
> And pluck the blossom where the wild bees hum;
> Then through the broomy bound with ease
>   they pass
> And press the sandy sheep-walk's slender grass
> Where dwarfish flowers among the gorse are
>   spread,
> And the lamb browses by the linnet's bed;
> Then 'cross the bounding brook they make
>   their way
> O'er its rough bridge—and there behold the
>   bay!
> The ocean smiling to the fervid sun—
> The waves that faintly fall and slowly run—
> The ships at distance and the boats at hand;
> And now they walk upon the sea-side sand,
> Counting the number and what kind they be,
> Ships softly sinking in the sleepy sea. . . .

But I must not continue. Crabbe has succeeded without any express mention or any use of what Ruskin calls " the pathetic fallacy," in making you see the scene through the eyes of the doomed man; has made you aware of the subconscious feeling which renders the dream and memory so intense. Scott seldom if ever attempts this; at most he hangs about the scene a little of the sadness of memory, as in the lines which close what I quoted on Blackford Hill:

> Nought do I see unchanged remain
> Save the rude cliffs and chiming brook.
> To me they make a heavy moan
> Of early friendships past and gone.

His sincerest feeling is uttered in the words, "Life could not be endured were it seen in reality." But in general, whatever the mood of the person in the story, it is his own enthusiastic love of scenery and Scotland that warms his descriptions, and it is this which made him, to Ruskin, the greatest of Nature poets: "And, first, observe Scott's habit of looking at nature neither as dead, or merely material, in the way that Homer regards it, nor as altered by his own feelings in the way that Keats and Tennyson regard it, but as having an animation and pathos of *its own*, wholly irrespective of human presence or passion —an animation which Scott loves and sympathises with, as he would with a fellow-creature, forgetting himself altogether, and subduing his own humanity before what seems to him the power of the landscape." And he goes on to quote the lines on the old thorn-tree in the letter to John Marriot prefixed to the second canto of *Marmion*.

But Scott has another link with Crabbe which Ruskin admires less. Speaking of his early attempts at description, Scott tells us that some association was always necessary to kindle his interest, some "alliance with moral feeling." Both he and Crabbe are prone to link a description with some didactic tag. Thus after the description of the scenery of *The Village* which I have quoted, Crabbe goes on:

> With mingled tints the rocky coasts abound,
> And a sad splendour hardly shines around.
> So looks the nymph whom wretched arts adorn,
> Betrayed by man then left for man to scorn;

> Whose cheek in vain assumes the mimic rose
> While her sad eyes the troubled breast disclose;
> Whose outward splendour is but folly's dress,
> Exposing most, when most it gilds distress.

Scott is rather fond of the same kind of moralising. The shadows of a mountain reflected in a lake

> ... lie
> Like future joys to fancy's eye.

Of a stream he comments:

> The foam-globes on her eddies ride
> Thick as the schemes of human pride
> That down life's current drive amain,
> As frail, as frothy, and as vain.

These and similar touches have nothing in common with either the pathetic fallacy, as in Tennyson's

> In the *dead unhappy* night and when the rain is on the roof,

or with the deeper reactions of a mind like Wordsworth's or Shelley's to the impression made on them by the life of Nature. They are survivals of the didacticism of the eighteenth century. "In all places of this kind," says Ruskin, "where a passing thought is suggested by some external scene, that thought is at once a slight and sad one. Scott's deeper moral sense is marked in the *conduct* of his stories, and in casual reflections or exclamations arising out of their plot, and therefore sincerely uttered; as that of Marmion:

> "Oh, what a tangled web we weave,
> When first we practise to deceive!"

SIR HERBERT GRIERSON

The same combination of warm and enthusiastic, rather than passionate, feeling and accuracy of detail which is characteristic of his descriptions of nature is obvious in many other features of the poems—in such details as his references to dogs (Scott might be called, says Adolphus, the Wilkie of dogs), his dialogue in its appropriateness to the persons concerned; and very notably in his descriptions of movement. Adolphus cites two passages, one descriptive of an approaching army, the other of the firing of a castle:

> Soon on the hill's steep verge he stood,
> That looks o'er Branksome's towers and wood;
> And martial murmurs, from below,
> Proclaim'd the approaching southern foe.
> Through the dark wood, in mingled tone,
> Were Border pipes and bugles blown;
> The coursers, neighing he could ken,
> A measured tread of marching men;
> While broke at times the solemn hum,
> The Almayn's sullen kettle-drum;
> And banners tall, of crimson sheen,
> Above the copse appear;
> And, glistening through the hawthorns green,
> Shine helm, and shield, and spear.
>
> Light forayers, first, to view the ground,
> Spurr'd their fleet coursers loosely round;
> Behind in close array, and fast,
> The Kendal archers, all in green,
> Obedient to the bugle blast,
> Advancing from the wood were seen.
>
> Then sudden, through the darken'd air
> A flash of lightning came;

> So broad, so bright, so red the glare,
> The castle seem'd on flame.
> Glanced every rafter of the hall,
> Glanced every shield upon the wall,
> Each trophied beam, each sculptured stone,
> Were instant seen, and instant gone;
> Full through the guests' bedazzled band
> Resistless flash'd the levin-brand,
> And fill'd the hall with smouldering smoke,
> As on the elvish page it broke;
> It broke, with thunder long and loud,
> Dismay'd the brave, appall'd the proud,—
> From sea to sea the larum rung;
> On Berwick wall, and at Carlisle withal,
> To arms the startled warders sprung.
> When ended was the dreadful roar,
> The elvish dwarf was seen no more!

In the narrative poems Scott has given rather freer expression to his own personal feelings than in the dramatic lyrics on which I have already touched. The principal place is, of course, the letters prefixed to each canto of *Marmion*. The strain of thought is a rather melancholy one in contrast to the enthusiastic flow of the narrative. "Of all poetry that I know," Ruskin writes, "none is so sorrowful as Scott's." Like Tennyson, he seems to be always haunted by the thought,

> All things are taken from us, and become
> Portions and parcels of the dreadful past.

It is the Minstrel's lament in the first of the narrative poems when he contrasts the unchanging flow of the River Teviot with the course of time:

> Unlike the tide of human time,
> Which, though it change in ceaseless flow,
> Retains each grief, retains each crime
> Its earliest course was doom'd to know;
> And, darker as it downward bears,
> Is stain'd with past and present tears;

and finds beautiful expression in the Spenserians which in like manner open and close the various cantos of *The Lady of the Lake*:

> Harp of the North, farewell! The hills grow dark,
> On purple peaks a deeper shade descending;
> In twilight copse the glow-worm lights her spark,
> The deer, half-seen, are to the covert wending.
> Resume thy wizard elm! the fountain lending,
> And the wild breeze, thy wilder minstrelsy;
> Thy numbers sweet with nature's vespers blending,
> With distant echo from the fold and lea,
> And herd-boy's evening pipe, and hum of housing bee.
>
> Yet, once again, farewell, thou minstrel harp!
> Yet, once again, forgive my feeble sway,
> And little reck I of the censure sharp
> May idly cavil at an idle lay.
> Much have I owed thy strains on life's long way,
> Through secret woes the world has never known,
> When on the weary night dawn'd wearier day,
> And bitterer was the grief devour'd alone.
> That I o'erlive such woes, Enchantress! is thine own.

A romantic story, but given a historical setting and told with an air of historical truth, romantic scenery and incidents vividly and truthfully described, a vein of feeling enthusiastic but touched with melancholy and always sincere. These seem to me the qualities which have given

Scott's tales a more enduring vitality than their more popular rivals at that time—Byron's more passionate stories of Turks and Greeks, or Moore's lighter *Lalla Rookh*, to say nothing of many forgotten imitations which slumber on the shelves of university libraries. But for this combination of romance and truth Scott was to find a medium that gave him greater freedom, more elbow-room than verse, and which allowed him to express a vein of humour which had hardly made itself evident in the verse tales.

Moreover, it is in the prose novels that Adolphus discovers the fullest evidence of the poet in Scott : " I do not now speak of detached thoughts, single expressions, or isolated passages ; the very conception and main structure of his stories is in some instances purely poetic. Take as an example the Bride of Lammermoor. Through the whole progress of that deeply affecting tale . . . we experience that fervour and exaltation of mind, that keen susceptibility of emotion, and that towering and perturbed state of the imagination, which poetry alone can produce."

II
HISTORY AND THE NOVEL

IN the fourth number of *The Rambler* (31st March 1750) Dr. Johnson wrote an essay, evoked by the publication of Smollett's *Roderick Random* in 1748 and Fielding's *Tom Jones* in 1749. The essay dealt with the new kind of novel inaugurated by Richardson's *Pamela* ten years earlier. " The works of fiction with which the present generation seem more particularly delighted, are such as exhibit life in its true state, diversified only by accidents that daily happen in the world, and influenced by passions and qualities which are really to be found in conversing with mankind. This kind of writing may be termed not improperly the comedy of romance, and is to be conducted nearly by the rules of comic poetry. Its province is to bring about natural events by easy means, and to keep up curiosities without the help of wonder. It is therefore precluded from the machines and expedients of the heroic romance, and can neither employ giants to snatch away a lady from the nuptial rites, nor knights to bring her back from captivity; it can neither bewilder its personages in deserts nor lodge them in imaginary castles."

Johnson goes on to describe the difficulties attending a fiction for which a real knowledge of life is required, and the responsibility of the author for the moral effect, especially on young readers, of life and character thus truthfully and vividly presented: "It is not a sufficient vindication of a character that it is drawn as it appears, for many characters ought never to be drawn: nor of a narrative that the train of events is agreeable to observation. What is called knowledge of the world will be found more frequently to make men cunning than good."

The type of novel described by Johnson has been with us ever since; and Anthony Trollope, in his *Autobiography*, agrees with Johnson that no form of literature has so powerful an influence on the minds of the young, shaping their expectations of what life has to offer, and forming for good or ill their ideals. But my subject is not the moral influence of the novel, which Scott recognises as clearly as Johnson. It is the history of the novel in the later eighteenth and early nineteenth century when this was affected by a revival of the demand for that element of wonder to which Johnson refers, of wonder awakening the sense of fear that attends upon any event which seems to transcend our normal experience. The period between 1765, when Horace Walpole published his *Castle of Otranto*, and the Waverley Novels witnessed the production of an extraordinary series of novels, enormously popular in their own day, hardly even by students readable to-day. The older type of novel did not, of course, cease. Fanny Burney's *Evelina* (1778) and *Cecilia* (1782) belong to these years, and Jane

Austen was preparing her fine work on the same line if keeping a satirical eye upon the romantic development which was producing the more popular stories.

The aim of the new type of novel, as described by Walpole and conceived by Scott also, was " to blend the two kinds of romance, the ancient and the modern. In the former, all was imagination and improbability; in the latter, nature is always intended to be, and sometimes has been, copied with success. Invention has not been wanting; but the great resources of fancy have been dammed up by a strict adherence to common life. . . . The author of the following pages thought it possible to reconcile the two kinds. Desirous of leaving the powers of fancy at liberty to expatiate through the boundless realms of invention, and thence of creating more interesting situations, he wished to conduct the mortal agents in his drama according to the rules of probability; in short, to make them think, speak, and act, as it might be supposed mere men and women would do in extraordinary positions." Walpole's aim was to bring the marvellous into real everyday life.

I need not recapitulate the history nor analyse the sources of the movement, such as the revival of an interest in our older literature and the Middle Ages—ballads and old romances, Gothic architecture, Chivalry and Catholicism. A great change in literature is often an index to a change in the audience addressed, and a possible factor in the change is that, with the initiation and growth of public libraries, readers for whom a knowledge of Richardson and Fielding was precluded by the high price of their works, and who were familiar through the chapbooks with older romance, were ready to appreciate a fiction which did not confine itself too strictly to the portrayal of real life and manners. The mass of people do not much care for a too realistic literature. To them literature is in the nature of an escape, and they welcome a romantic portrayal of life whether from Mrs. Anne Radcliffe or Miss Marie Corelli.

The name now generally given to this group is the " Terror Novel." A recent study has divided them into various subdivisions which frequently overlap with one another. There are the " Gothic Romances," those namely which move around some Gothic castle, as is indicated by the names of a number of them,—*The Castle of Otranto*, *Ivey Castle*, *The Solitary Castle*, *The Haunted Castle*, *The Castle on the Rock*, *The Castles of Athlin and Dunbayne*, the last a Highland story by Mrs. Radcliffe, who knew nothing about the Highlands. A second class is that of " Historical Romances," in which real historical characters are made to figure,—*Haunted Castle, a Norman Romance*; *The Anglo-Saxons, or the Court of Ethelwulf, a Romance*; *A Peep at our Ancestors*; *The Wolf of Badenoch*, etc., etc. A third division contains " Romances of Magicians and Devils," of which the German poet Schiller was the inaugurator by his *Der Geisterseher*. It was translated into English in 1795. English examples are *The*

Necromancers, or The Tale of the Black Forest; *St. Leon, A Tale of the Sixteenth Century* (this last by William Godwin). Godwin's son-in-law, Shelley, wrote in early days *St. Irvyne, or The Rosicrucian*, and James Hogg wrote *The Brownie of Bodsbeck*; and there are many others. In a fourth class come " Ghost Romances," for which Schiller again leads the way. Here comes Mrs. Radcliffe's most famous novel *The Mysteries of Udolpho*; and some other titles are *Tales of Terror, or More Ghosts*; *The Priory of St. Claire, or the Spectre of the Murdered Nun*; etc., etc. To a fifth class my authority assigns the name of " Anticlerical Romances." It would be juster to call them " Anti-Roman Romances," for the feeling which inspires them is not so much sceptical as the Protestant distrust of monks, nuns, priests, the Inquisition, etc., etc. The leading and best known example in this class is M. G. Lewis's *The Monk* (1795), which is more readable than one expects. Mrs. Radcliffe contributed *The Italian, or The Confessional of the Black Penitent* (1797); *St. Margaret's Cave, or The Nun's Story*, *The Mysterious Penitent, Horrors of Oakendale Abbey*, etc., are a few more significant names. Finally there are " Robber Romances," inspired by Schiller's *Die Räuber*. Lewis contributed *The Bravo of Venice*, Miss Jane Porter *The Scottish Chiefs*, and a certain Miss Smith *The Caledonian Bandit*; and there are endless others. None of these types died out quickly. They were being produced during and after Scott's lifetime. The greatest of Gothic Romances is, after all, Victor

Hugo's *Notre-Dame de Paris*. Anthony Trollope's mother was in 1847 the author of *Father Eustace, a Tale of the Jesuits*. Ainsworth, G. P. R. James, and W. H. Kingston were authors of robber novels which I read when young, and I have no doubt that boys still read stories which in one way or another play upon the nerves of wonder and apprehension. As Scott says: " Curiosity and a lurking love of mystery, together with a germ of superstition, are more general ingredients in the human mind, and more widely diffused through the mass of humanity, than either genuine taste for the comic or true feeling of the pathetic."

What, then, was Scott's own reaction to the fiction of the day, realistic and romantic? He had been a reader of novels in his youth, but not an indiscriminate reader: " My desk usually contained a store of most miscellaneous volumes, especially works of fiction of every kind, which were my supreme delight. I might except novels, unless those of the better and higher class, for though I read many of them, yet it was with more selection than might have been expected. The whole Jemmy and Jenny Jessamy tribe I abhorred, and it required the art of Burney, or the feeling of Mackenzie, to fix my attention upon a domestic tale. But all that was adventurous and romantic I devoured without discrimination. . . . Every thing that touched on knight-errantry was particularly acceptable to me, and I soon attempted to imitate what I so greatly admired. My efforts, however, were in the manner of the tale-teller, not of the bard "; and he goes on to relate how he and a friend entertained each other with stories in their walks together. Of the content of these stories we know nothing, for, if we may believe him, it was not till about the end of the century that he made his first effort to compose " a tale of chivalry " which was to be in the style of *The Castle of Otranto*, with plenty of Border characters and supernatural incidents. A small fragment of this story, called *Thomas the Rhymer*, and of another, are printed in the general introduction to the first collected edition of the Waverley Novels. In or about 1805 he wrote the early, autobiographical chapters of *Waverley* as introductory to a novel on the Highlands. But this was laid aside, its place being taken by *The Lady of the Lake*. But *Waverley, or 'Tis Sixty Years Since*, was among the works advertised as forthcoming in the years 1809–10. It would almost seem that the Highland novel and the Highland poem proceeded *pari passu*, though it was not until 1814 that the novel was finally completed and published. Meantime in 1807–8 Scott had revised and concluded an antiquarian novel by Joseph Strutt, *Queenhoo-Hall*.

It is thus quite possible that Scott might have joined the throng of terror and wonder novelists as a rival to Mrs. Radcliffe and " Monk " Lewis. Indeed, if one considers, one can discover the features of all the groups mentioned above in the Waverley Novels. There are Gothic castles and ruined abbeys, historical characters, and ghosts, magicians and criminals, but in consequence of the local setting and historical perspective they become natural features in a quite probable story. For there was another side to Scott's mind and his study. " To the romances and poetry, in which I chiefly delighted, I had always added the study of history, especially as connected with military events. . . . Familiar acquaintance with the specious miracles of fiction brought with it some degree of satiety, and I began by degrees to seek in history, memoirs, voyages and travels, and the like, events nearly as wonderful as those which were the work of imagination, with the additional advantage that they were at least in a great measure true." It was this combination in Scott's mind of a solid knowledge of and interest in archaeology and history on the one hand, and of romantic fiction on the other, which made him finally the creator of the historical novel, a novel which should give the same sense of reality as those of Fielding and Smollett but whose subjects should be events taken from past history and those of a romantic character. Moreover there is one novelist whom I have not mentioned who had opened a way which Scott was to follow; that is, Maria Edgeworth in her novels of provincial Irish life.

Scott had, of course, precursors in what might be called historical drama and romance,—the romances of the seventeenth century, such as *Le Grand Cyrus*, *Cassandre*, etc., the historical plays of Shakespeare in this country, of Corneille and Racine in France, and the ostensibly historical novels to which I have referred. Wherein do

Scott's historical novels differ from the works of his predecessors? From Shakespeare, indeed, Scott learned a great deal. It was from *Henry IV* and *Henry V* that he learned the art of combining historical characters and scenes with scenes and characters of low life and comedy,— Falstaff, Ancient Pistol, Bardolph, the Hostess, etc. But whatever may be true of the kings and princes in these plays, the comic characters do not belong to the age of Henry IV or Henry V but to that of Queen Elizabeth. An historical novelist of to-day who chose the reign of Henry IV as the setting of his story would have gone for his humorous characters to Chaucer's Prologue to the *Canterbury Tales*, and given us pardoners, friars, and somnours instead of swaggering soldiers and haunters of the theatre. The heroes of Corneille and Racine are Frenchmen of the age of Louis XIV. The historical romances of Mrs. Radcliffe and her imitators are even less historical in atmosphere, manners, and character. " In *The Mysteries of Udolpho*, a story dealing with events of the year 1584, Parisian fashions, French opera, and French manners are spoken of as dominating in the world." The characters have the elegance and sensibility which were the fashion of the later eighteenth century, One thing, however, Mrs. Radcliffe did contribute to the romantic historical novel, which Scott was to use freely alike in his narrative poems and his novels; that is, local scenery. Indeed it is the scenic setting which perhaps more than anything else distinguishes the historical novel of this period from all preceding novels, and has proved its most enduring legacy to subsequent novels. The older novel of character and manners, of Fielding and Smollett, takes both scenery and time for granted—the country and the period are those of writer and reader—so that, except to make clear the course of the story, no description is required: but in Scott's stories, whether in verse or in prose, the reader must always be made aware of the place and the time; must catch a glimpse of Melrose by moonlight, of Edinburgh and the Firth of Forth and the coast of Fife from Blackford Hill; must see the Teviot winding its silver course, or feel himself among the lakes and heather hills of the Highlands.

This, as I have said, is the most important legacy from the novels of this period, for the scenic setting, as you can see in a moment, is an element by no means necessarily confined to an historical novel. In the work of every novelist since Scott's day the scenic environment has become a more or less necessary part of the whole impression produced by the novel. A French critic complained that in Victor Hugo's *Notre-Dame* the background tends to become more important than the characters. In Balzac's novels how much depends on the setting,—descriptions of the interiors of houses as well as of city and country. Dickens has the same delight in interiors and a recurring background to his stories is to be found in the streets of London, the River Thames, its wharves and its muddy banks. George Meredith's fields and roads and sunny or showery weather are conceived and presented in the spirit and manner of the poet. The district of the Potteries is an essential feature in the stories of Arnold Bennett; the very name of Marcel Proust's great novel points to this dominant interest in places and local colour.

But you must be aware of the time—of the epoch. This is the most crucial requirement of all, and that in which Scott's predecessors had most obviously either made no effort to achieve success, or failed to do so. One man indeed had made the effort but had done so too entirely in the spirit of a didactic antiquarian. In editing and completing his work Scott learned one or two necessary conditions of success. You must not attempt a too exact picture in every detail. As regards the language, for example, there is a strict limit to the measure of archaic colour which you can venture to lend to your style. But this feature, which Flaubert calls the *frisson historique*, Huizinga " the historical sensation," is what the novelist is most anxious to procure, and about it centres the whole question of the legitimacy (you might say) of the historical novel.

Can the novelist reproduce the spirit and form of a past age with an effect that is not only vivid but trustworthy ? Within certain historical limits this is perhaps possible, and one of the most important factors will be the style in which the story is written. Speaking of Thackeray's *Henry Esmond*, G. K. Chesterton writes : " It is marvellous that a man apparently so casual and conversational . . . should have written so many thousand words and so thick a book without using one word that might not have been used at the court of Queen Anne." It is as you go farther back, when any attempt to reproduce the language becomes impossible, that difficulties accumulate. It is sufficient, Scott came to the conclusion, to give to your language a little of the colour of that of our grandparents, a slightly archaic tint; and even that leads too easily to what Stevenson dubbed " tushery " because the characters are apt to repeat too often some phrase such as " tush, quoth he." For the rest you must depend on description, character, sentiment, and manners; and how difficult it is to do this with real accuracy! For a work which is to be read just as a novel it does not really much matter as long as we get some impression of a past age. We have had since Scott's day some elaborate but probably illusory pictures of past epochs— brilliant *tours de force* such as Flaubert's *Salammbô*, Señor Larreta's *The Glory of Don Ramiro*, and not a few recent novels, English, American, and German. What has brought the historical novel under suspicion of late has been its effect on history and biography. Carlyle was the first to recognise the importance of the Waverley Novels for the writer of history. "These Historical Novels have taught all men this truth . . . that the bygone ages of the world were actually filled by living men, not by protocols, state-papers, controversies, and abstractions of men. Not abstractions were they, not diagrams and theorems; but men, in buff or other coats and breeches, with colour in their cheeks, with passion in their stomach, and the idioms, features and vitalities of very men. It is a little word this; inclusive of great meaning! History will henceforth have to take thought of it." And so Carlyle set himself to supply in his *French Revolution* a kind of third dimension to history—to write what is not merely an account of the facts and an indication of the general causes at work, but is a vivid picture of the individuals and of the stormy surface of life as seen by those who lived at that time. Carlyle had many followers in ways of their own—Macaulay, Motley, Prescott, and such French historians as Guizot and Michelet. Indeed, some recent critics of the aim and art of history have declared that such a picture as Carlyle endeavoured to give, is the proper aim of history: " The historian must recreate for us the past; and this can be done only on condition that he makes it possible for us to relive the individual event in its individual happening . . . he will . . . demand of the hero or reader that he reproduce in his imagination a piece of actuality " (Rickert, *Kulturwissenschaft und Naturwissenschaft*, 1894). " The final goal of the historian is always to recreate the genuine form of the past with vital vivid clearness. What history offers is pictures of men and human life with all the wealth of their developments preserved in individual liveliness " (Windelband, *Geschichte der Naturwissenschaft*). So Rickert and Windelband; but others are dubious of the possibility of achieving such an effect without an element of deception. The vivid sense of the past, what Flaubert calls the *frisson historique*, is something that can be caught at moments, but only at moments. It is in the nature of what the Germans call *Ahnung*, a divination, caught from some accidental contact—it may be a line from an old song, or a contemporary chronicle like that of Salimbene. Carlyle tells us of the vivid impression made on his mind by a trifling incident which Clarendon relates, when describing the escape of Charles II after the battle of Worcester. To attempt to elaborate such an impression into anything like a complete picture of the time is to run the risk of falsification. The aim of the historian is somewhat different; it is to set forth as truly as he can what actually happened and how it came about, to render intelligible the interconnection of events.

History, I am told, is suffering at this moment from two perils, is being invaded and perverted from two sides—from the side of biological science and from that of literature. Historians have taken over from biology the conception of evolution and speak of historical phenomena—a civilisation, a constitution, a revolution—as though these were organisms like a mouse or a tree of a specific type, from a study of which we can deduce certain laws applicable to other cases. " Modern examples are the pseudo-history of Spengler, where the individual historical facts which he calls culture are frankly conceived as natural products growing and perishing with the same superb aimlessness as the flowers of the field" (R. G. Collingwood, *Human Nature and Human History*).

But history is threatened from another side—the literary. "There is nothing disloyal in this. Literature is, just as much as science, a characteristic of culture. The function of literature is not merely to write pretty poems and tales, but to make the world intelligible. . . . The value of literature lies in the representative, the symbolic activity of the characters, not in the controlling charm of genuineness, of the ' this did actually so occur ' " (Huizinga, *Cultur-Historische Verkenningen*). In short, as Aristotle said long ago, the concern of the poet is not with what did actually happen, but with what might happen now or might have happened at such or such a definite period of history, so far as we have acquired a sufficient knowledge and understanding of the period in question.

The question has been made acute by the emergence of a hybrid form which claims to be history while it is in fact literature. The historian, concerned for truth, cannot present his material with the definite, intelligible, vivid clearness which readers enjoy; and accordingly, encouraged by publishers, the amateur steps in, the man with a flair for the taste of the public, and gives you literature professing to be history. The tone of such work is determined by the taste of the day. In the eighteenth century what was generally required in a biography was a moralising tone, a respect for virtue. In the sympathetic life of his friend Savage, Johnson does not spare his faults or forget to read a moral lesson: "The reigning error of his life was that he mistook the love for the practice of virtue, and was indeed not so much a good man as the friend of goodness." The taste of readers to-day is different. As Huizinga puts it: "No balancing of good and evil is required. Passion alone is enough, or what passes for passion. In every rendering of actuality by word or image . . . the element of passion must be exaggerated. Moral standards are absolutely not to be commended. Venturous spirits are assured of an aureole from the modern world by doing homage to immorality. This homage is as much a form of cultural hypocrisy as a hypocritically virtuous tone could be." To this tendency we owe what has been called the *vie romancée* which writes the life of the hero as though the author were familiar with every detail of his daily actions and conversations.

Scott did not thus confound history and the historical romance. He wrote both history and biography, much in the manner of Dr. Johnson, sober narrative with occasional moralising. His romances made no pretence to be history. He took, in fact, the greatest liberty with facts and dates. They were a novelist's and poet's picture of how things might have been in such and such a period. As such they differ greatly in the degree to which they give us a convincing impression of producing the illusion of being the picture of life in a past age. Quite recently I read a short novel, *Tropic Rome*, by a Mr. Dennis Lacaid, which gave what seemed to me a brilliant picture of what Goa might have been in the day of her rule by a decadent Spain. The success of such studied reproductions depends mainly on two things—a great deal of vivid description (Goa is still there for study), and an effort, never more than partly successful, to suggest passions and manners strikingly different from our own; and the easiest way to do this is to exaggerate the elements of passion and violence. In Señor Larreta's novel the author writes as though he himself were living in the age of Philip II and shared its feelings, subscribed to its moral standards, insomuch that debauchery and even murder seemed to the hero trifling and venial sins compared with the fact that he has condoned heresy and shown mercy to Jews. The *Jew Süss* and *The Ugly Duchess* of Lion Feuchtwanger are written in the same heightened tone. Scott does not do this. He never lets us forget that he and we are living in a more enlightened age, and are looking back from our moral and social position on the past which he is describing. In *Thaïs* and *La Tentation de Saint Antoine* Anatole France and Flaubert have produced by a subtle blend of learning, imagination, psychology and irony an effect which Scott only once approaches, and that along a line of simpler, if sounder, psychology in the blind fiddler's tale in *Redgauntlet*. But even Scott's own *Ivanhoe* seemed to contemporary reviewers a story that " requires to be read with a quite new and much greater effort of imagination than its precursors, the manners being unlike anything either the author or the reader of the present times could have had any opportunity of knowing by personal observation."

The fact is that Scott's chief interest was not either description for its own sake or manners just as manners. "A tale of manners," he writes, " to be interesting, must either refer to antiquity ... or it must bear a vivid reflection of those scenes which are passing daily before our eyes." It is accordingly in such experiments as *Ivanhoe* and *Count Robert of Paris* that we get the most carefully drawn picture and the most antiquarian study of manners. Manners and description are, in his best novels, subordinate to, interwoven with, his chief interest, which is incident, character and feeling. His aim was to throw " the force of my narrative upon the characters and passions of the actors;—those passions common to men in all stages of society, and which have alike agitated the human heart, whether it throbbed under the steel corslet of the fifteenth century " or any other costume.

Historically Scott is most successful when the story is placed in a period which was not for him entirely past, the spirit of which was still to a greater or lesser extent active. He is not successful in purely mediaeval tales, as *The Monastery, The Abbot, The Fair Maid of Perth*; for, among other things, he did not understand the Catholicism of those centuries, the spirit—to say nothing of Dante—of Chaucer, who can with equal naturalism and sincerity tell a secular, even a coarse, story and the story of a saint. We are apt to read into these pious tales a note of amused scepticism which was, I believe, foreign to the poet. It is in the seventeenth and eighteenth centuries that Scott is most at home. It may be that, as Lockhart says, *Old Mortality* was the first of the novels in which he ventured outside of what he could still, personally or through other people still alive, remember; but he was familiar with the religious temper of that century, for it was still alive and active in Edinburgh and George Square. *Waverley*, *The Antiquary*, *Guy Mannering*, *The Heart of Midlothian*, *Rob Roy*, *The Bride of Lammermoor*, *A Legend of Montrose*, *Redgauntlet*—all these deal with a time the spirit and passions of which were only passing away in Scott's own life-time. The tug between Presbyterianism and Prelacy, between Covenanter and Royalist, the new interests—social, intellectual, political—which were pervading Scottish life as the eighteenth century gave way to the nineteenth, all these were in the air which he breathed. How people had felt and thought in the sixteenth century when Catholic and Protestant first found themselves face to face, he only partly divines; and his pictures of even older times, are, like those of other novelists, necessarily somewhat artificial and illusory.

Yet in some of these more artificially or artfully constructed stories of a past which is no longer his own—*Ivanhoe*, *Kenilworth*, *The Fortunes of Nigel*, even *Count Robert of Paris*—he has managed to create some memorable characters: Rebecca and the Templar in *Ivanhoe*,

Queen Elizabeth in *Kenilworth*, James I of England in *The Fortunes of Nigel*, Louis XI in *Quentin Durward*. Whether historically correct or not, these are individual and living characters.

Lastly, there are those characters which belong to no age or every age—gentlemen, bourgeois, the peasantry and the poor. What a procession they form: Baron Bradwardine and Davie Gellatley, Colonel Mannering and Dominie Sampson and Meg Merrilies, Oldbuck and Edie Ochiltree, Jeanie Deans and Madge Wildfire—there is no end to the number of vivid, natural, individual characters. There are sides of human character which he has not touched. As Adolphus justly contends, he has failed in scenes of " bold and unmitigated vulgarity." There is nothing to compare with the reckless joviality of Burns's " Jolly Beggars ". His picture of the poor is generally kindly, but, as occasional passages show, he is quite aware both of their capacity for malignity and their sense of injustice. His stories have at times suffered from his own or James Ballantyne's anxiety to please the public by a happy ending, so that the tragic potentiality of such stories as *Old Mortality* and *St. Ronan's Well* is left undeveloped.

Scott's closest affinities are, after all, not with the romantic and terror novels of his age but with the older masters, Fielding and Smollett, and perhaps most of all with the great Spaniard whom he so much admired, the author of *Don Quixote*. There is the same genial humanity in both, the same subtle blend of realism and poetry, of fact and the transfiguring imagination. For the poet in Scott is more obvious in the great moments of the novels than in any narrative poems,—in Meg Merrilies's denunciation of the laird of Ellangowan, in Brown's recognition in the same story of the place and the song recalled from his infant years. Jeanie Deans's appeal to the Queen is worthy in its way of comparison with the speech which Shakespeare put into the mouth of Marc Antony. Careless and open as Scott's prose is, he ever and anon gives to what he says a touch that only a poet could. One might, I sometimes fancy, divide writers of to-day into those who refuse and denounce, and those who accept and enjoy, human nature and human life: Ibsen, Hardy, and many of the Russian and French novelists and their followers; while on the other side are the inheritors of the genial kindly humanity of a Chaucer, a Cervantes, a Scott. Which is the better, each reader must decide for himself.

EDWIN MUIR
1944

Reprinted from
The University of Edinburgh Journal, 1945
Vol. XIII, No. 2

I

WALTER SCOTT: THE MAN

I should begin by expressing the sense of mingled honour and disadvantage which I feel in being asked to follow Sir Herbert Grierson as a lecturer on Scott. The honour I need not enlarge upon in this place; the disadvantage is equally obvious: for Sir Herbert is, I suppose, the chief authority on Scott now living, and I am only an admirer and periodical reader of that great novelist. Before preparing these lectures I re-read the two lectures which Sir Herbert gave a little more than four years ago. I was filled with admiration for the fine critical discrimination and the easy learning displayed in them, and the feeling they gave me that here someone was speaking who was a master of his subject. I cannot hope to emulate such a performance.

My own treatment of Scott will be much more amateurish and impressionistic; I shall be concerned chiefly with some things in his character and work that puzzle and disconcert me. And first of all with a feeling I have often had after re-reading him. I experience the full shock of his imagination, but in a while I find it has left no lasting echo. Certain scenes and characters remain, along with a sense of abounding stir and bustle; but the full impact of a great mind, changing and illuminating one's sense of life, is not there. Or rather, after being present while I read, it is dissipated. In one of his lectures Sir Herbert Grierson quoted a contemporary of Scott as saying that he had not " the gift of suggesting, as some poets can, by a few details far more than meets the eye, because they communicate an emotional impression which of itself helps to evoke the completer picture." The critic was speaking of Scott's poetry; but his observation applies also to the world of imagination described in the Waverley Novels. They do not bring that quickening to the mind which sets the mind going by itself, as the work of lesser novelists such as Sterne and Thackeray and Jane Austen does. They do not go on working within us long after we have read them.

What reason can be found for this peculiarity of Scott's imagination? The most obvious one is a certain lack of intimacy. By universal testimony Scott was a frank and open-hearted man; but frankness has nothing to do with intimacy in this sense. Wordsworth was not frank, nor was Emily Brontë; yet both are intimate writers in a sense that Scott was not. For intimacy does not consist in a writer's telling us all about himself, but rather in communicating entire, with scrupulous fidelity, what his imagination reveals to him about life, whether it is pleasing or displeasing. Scott chose to keep something back; he lacked the overpowering compulsion. A writer who gives his imaginative vision entire must have a devotion to his work, the deliberate devotion of Wordsworth, or the instinctive devotion of Emily Brontë; and he must prize certain invisible things above the practical things of life. It is hard to judge how far Scott did this. He certainly was not devoted to his art as Wordsworth and Keats were, or even as Dickens and Thackeray were. The difficulty is to know to what he was chiefly devoted.

It has been said of Scott that he was too busy living to have much time or energy for writing. This is one of these absurd apologies which do him more harm than good. Yet we know that in his prime he liked to be ten hours a day outdoors, shooting, fishing or riding. John Buchan in his biography also insists that " we shall not understand Scott unless we realize how much he lived in a secret world of his own, an inner world of dream and memory, from which he brought great treasures." And a little later Buchan mentions quite a different side of him in saying that he " liked the idea of marriage as a step in that progress in life to which one side of him (his father's side) was vowed." The progress in life again, the getting-on, had to find some palpable symbol; that symbol was Abbotsford, a house which was equally suited to a great Border laird and a great Gothic novelist. Abbotsford in turn had to be kept up, and now and then enlarged; this involved the making of money on a great scale, and money could be made on a great scale only by writing rapidly one story after another. Finally even that was not sufficient; Scott needed money in still greater plenty, and, without the necessary training or aptitude, involved himself in a maze of business transactions. In this chaos of activities, his hunting and riding, his responsibilities as a country gentleman and a Border laird, his money-making, his writing, his social engagements in Edinburgh, his secret life of dream and memory, where did his main devotion lie? The question becomes still harder to answer when we reflect that two of the lives he led, his writing life, and his business life, he kept secret for many years. He was frank and open-hearted; but a frank and open-hearted man who keeps two of his lives secret, and cherishes in addition a secret world of his own of which even his published work shows few traces; a man of acknowledged good sense who squanders his health and finally his life to realise a fantastic dream, is a very difficult man to understand. Such riddles do not await our solution, but at most our respectful consideration; there can be no *explanation* of Scott or of anyone else; if an explanation were forthcoming we should not know what to do with it; it would be useless; we should have to turn from it again to Scott himself.

But to establish within the circumference of the riddle some connections between Scott's character and his work should be possible. One of them is obvious enough. To writers of Scott's creative genius the practical activities in which they engage, however apparently irrelevant, are generally transformed into subject-matter for their imagination; even their errors and misfortunes are somehow turned to account. The same impulse which drove Scott to build Abbotsford enabled him to understand the man of ambition and the palpable form and bounds of a dream of earthly glory. Without his active hours in the open air he could not have described so convincingly men's enjoyment in exercising their physical powers. Even his business speculations must have helped him to realise by what curiously mixed ways the ambitious man achieves that respect and power which, seen from outside, appear to be quite without alloy.

In the discussion of *Hamlet* in Joyce's *Ulysses* the author makes John Eglinton say of Shakespeare's marriage to Anne Hathaway and his desertion of her afterwards, " The world believes that Shakespeare made a mistake and got out of it as quickly and as best he could," to which Stephen Dedalus replies, " Bosh! A man of genius makes no mistakes. His errors are volitional and are the portals of discovery." This is the pure artist's point of view affirmed with fanatical conviction by a man who was resolved to put all his own mistakes into his work, and all the knowledge, pleasant and unpleasant, which they brought him. Scott's conception of his art was very different from Joyce's, and his estimation of his genius much less arrogant; he accepted it and the delight it gave him, one imagines, very much as he accepted his delightful hours in the open air. Abbotsford no doubt became in time a portal of discovery; but it is certain that he did not regard it as such. And his mistakes, no matter how much he may have learned from them as a man and a novelist, remained mistakes in his eyes, whether volitional or not.

But whatever else went into his work, there was one episode in his life which never did so, or at best in the most shadowy and ghostlike way—his unsuccessful love affair as a young man with Williamina Stuart-Belsches, whose marriage to another suitor threw him into such despair that his friends were concerned for his life. We have evidence enough that his rejection by Williamina caused him lasting grief. While he was courting her he had cut her name on the turf beside the castle gate at St. Andrews. Thirty-four years later, sitting on an adjacent gravestone, he wondered why the name should still agitate his heart. A few months afterwards he met Lady Jane, Williamina's mother, in Edinburgh; Williamina had then been dead for seventeen years. " I . . . fairly softened myself like an old fool," he wrote, " with recalling old stories, till I was fit for nothing but shedding tears and repeating verses for the whole night. This is sad work. The very grave gives up its dead, and time rolls back thirty years to add to my perplexities." After her marriage he had resolutely banished Williamina from his thoughts, but in spite of him she invaded his secret world, for it is said that on the eve of any great misfortune she appeared to him in his dreams.

In the summer after Williamina's marriage Scott's heart was " handsomely pieced," as he put it, by a young lady whom he met during a visit to the English Lakes. Miss Charlotte Margaret Carpenter became his wife. Twelve years later he wrote to Lady Abercorn: " Mrs. Scott's match and mine was of our own making, and proceeded from the most sincere affection on both sides, which has rather increased than diminished during twelve years' marriage. But it was something short of love in all its forms, which I suspect people only feel once in their lives; folks who have been nearly drowned in bathing rarely venturing a second time out of their depth." Unlike Williamina, Mrs. Scott never entered his secret world.

This episode which Scott put so resolutely behind him but which refused to be banished altogether, filling him with agitation thirty years later when the object of his love was dead, making him prefer affection to love as a basis of marriage, was clearly one of the decisive experiences in his life. It is useless to speculate now what would have happened if Williamina had returned his love instead of rejecting it; yet one can hardly resist it. If he had found happiness with Williamina would Abbotsford have become so important to him, would his ambition have fixed itself on such a limited and yet ostentatious object, would his ten hours a day in the open air have been so dear to him? And might not the development of his genius have been different, might not his imagination have acquired a greater intimacy from his experience of the most intimate of all human relations? In any case, the effect of her rejection of him was to make him turn away from one potentiality of experience for good. Yet as he was, on one side, a lover of adventure, like his heroes, the desire to venture out of his depth could not be eradicated so easily; he could not rid himself of it by marrying for affection instead of for love. He had to venture out of his depth, and he did so in financial speculation. It was in business that he indulged his need for adventure.

A natural reticence in Scott, confirmed by the literary and moral conventions of his time, prevented him from recreating in imagination the story of his early love. Or perhaps the memory was so painful that he could not bear to evoke it. John Buchan praises him for this abstention, but it seems to be a matter neither for praise nor for blame; we do not blame Shakespeare for his Sonnets. Scott was not devoted to the art of writing with the fanaticism of a modern novelist like Joyce, nor prepared to offer up to it his buried secrets. Nevertheless it is possible that Joyce's generalisation has a certain point if we apply it to Scott's resolve to put the memory of Williamina behind him; for it was probably the main reason for his inability to portray love, and for the great number of insipid female figures in his novels. His old women, his peasant women, his queens and princesses, his gipsies and vagabonds, all of them by virtue of age or class unlikely to prove dangerous to any of the young heroes in whom we see an image of Scott himself at the stage when he was in love with Williamina, are drawn with a sure hand. The others, the potentially dangerous ones, seem to fall in love because in a romance they are expected to do so; and their love stories would quickly weary us, and Scott too, if they were not enlivened with all sorts of intrigues and dangers.

It seems plausible to think, then, that the disastrous outcome of Scott's affair with Williamina and the resolution with which he put her memory behind him contracted the scope of his imagination and made it impossible for him to describe love. It may have been, too, the cause of his general lack of intimacy. For some reason he could not say the most intimate thing of all, the thing which might have given him the gift " of suggesting by a few details far more than meets the eye, because they communicate an emotional impression which of itself helps to evoke the completer picture." The emotional impression is lacking. He would always have been one of the great objective writers. But, if the course of his life had been different, he might have conveyed in his picture of life a more profound sense of significance. The bustle, the energy, the humour and pathos of life are there as they are nowhere else, even in Balzac and Tolstoy, but there is no high criticism of life. When Scott expresses a serious judgment of experience it comes from the secret world where the memory of Williamina was buried, and its burden is that all is vanity, the bustle, the adventure, the glory, everything that he created with such genial warmth and abundance:

> Look not thou on beauty's charming,
> Sit thou still when kings are arming . . .

> Stop thine ear against the singer,
> From the red gold keep thy finger—
> Vacant heart, and hand, and eye,
> Easy live and quiet die.

If we are conscious of an emptiness beneath the bustle and action of his novels, and beneath the surface of his busy life, the reason may be here.

The affair with Williamina may possibly throw some light on another trait of Scott—his grossly practical attitude to his writings, which is like that of a man who turns from a high satisfaction to make sure of a lower one. In the introductory epistle to *The Fortunes of Nigel* he speaks very frankly:

> No one shall find me rowing against the stream. I care not who knows it—I write for general amusement. . . . A man should strike while the iron is hot, and hoist sail while the wind is fair. If a successful author keep not the stage, another instantly takes his ground.

If we accept that statement at its face value, we shall be forced to think that Scott had no aim but success. Yet " I care not who knows it " implies at least that he was not proud of what he was saying. And he softens the effect of his declaration later by a more plausible explanation of his hurried and careless method of composition:

> I should be chin-deep in the grave, man, before I had done with my task, and, in the meanwhile, all the quirks and quiddities which I might have devised for my reader's amusement, would lie rotting in my gizzard.

The creations of his imagination crowded in upon

him so thick and fast that he had to deal with them as best he could.

Yet there was a genuine reason for his determination to keep the stage and not resign it to the next comer; for he was always in need of money, since he was driven by another impulse just as powerful as his imagination, the ambition whose symbol was Abbotsford. Ambition on a large scale generally involves the taking of risks. He himself was adventurous on one side and prudent on another, as befitted the son of an impulsive and imaginative mother and a respectable and practical father. In his life these two sides of him seem to have played a complicated game of hide-and-seek with each other. As a writer he lived in a secret world of romance and adventure, while to his acquaintances he existed as a respectable gentleman of means. The curious thing is that it was the romancer and adventurer who produced the means, and the respectable gentleman who squandered them. One does not know whether to regard Abbotsford as the unrealisable dream of the romancer, or the final justification of the man of position. There is a stage in Scott's life after which it is almost impossible to disentangle his business and social from his literary activities, for they fall into the position of cause and effect, the income from his novels paying his debts, and the dream of Abbotsford forcing him to get still more deeply into debt. The romantic world he created in his books became a sort of bank from which he drew the credit to realise the ideal of a splendid traditional Border community with himself at its head. If he had succeeded in realising that ideal it would probably have satisfied both sides of him, the romantic and the social.

In this confusion of activities which makes up Scott's life as a man, where each activity seems to be performing a function better suited to the others, where writing is regarded as a means of making money and business turns out to be a means of losing it, we are brought up once more against his regardless attitude to his genius. His genius and his ambition pulled him in opposite directions. His ambition was not to be known as a great writer, but to achieve a distinguished position in society and to live a life of traditional grandeur in the Border country and of social influence in Edinburgh. Wordsworth did not know that division, nor on a different level did Dickens; their genius and their ambition were set in the same direction; they put all of themselves into their work; they had no Abbotsford.

There remains Scott's secret world into which Williamina found her way, and no one else so far as we know. When he draws upon it its message is unmistakable and tells us that all action is vain, as in Lucy's song in *The Bride of Lammermoor*, or predetermined by absolute necessity, as in Redgauntlet's outburst on liberty of choice. It is concerned with death and the grave, as in " Proud Maisie " and the conversation between the old women in the churchyard when the Master of Ravenswood rides away. These are the voices of his secret world. Is it fanciful to imagine that they bring us back again to Williamina Stuart-Belsches, who still existed in his secret world although she was dead, and was twice dead to him through her first rejection of him? Among the novels, there is most of his secret world in *The Bride of Lammermoor*, which he wrote in a delirium of pain, so that he could not remember a single scene when it was shown to him and found the whole " monstrous gross and grotesque." In some of his later novels there is evidence that he had accepted consciously its pessimistic reading of life, his physical powers and his vast capacity for enjoyment having by then declined. There is the passage towards the end of *Woodstock*: " Years rush by us like the wind. We see not whence the eddy comes, nor whitherward it is tending, and we seem ourselves to witness their flight without a sense that we are changed; and yet Time is beguiling man of his strength as the wind robs the woods of their foliage." There is Redgauntlet's outburst on free-will: " The privilege of free action belongs to no mortal—we are tied down by the fetters of duty—our mortal path is limited by the regulations of honour—our most indifferent actions are meshes of the web of destiny by which we are all surrounded. . . . Yes, young man, in doing and suffering we play but the part allotted to us by Destiny, the manager of this strange drama—stand bound to act no more than is prescribed, to say no more than is set down for us; and yet we mouth about free-will, and freedom of thought and action, as if Richard must not die, or Richmond conquer, exactly where the Author has decreed it shall be so."

This is the comment of Scott's secret world on the world of bustling action. What gives *Redgauntlet* a unique place among the Waverley Novels is that it shows us a man of action aware of the vanity of action, who continues the fight in spite of that knowledge, " tied down by the fetters of duty," " limited by the regulations of honour." Compared with him Scott's other heroes live in a world of illusion. Their world is more rich and various and coloured and in a sense more full of interest than Redgauntlet's predetermined world. It is the world which Scott most enjoyed describing; but to one who knew Redgauntlet's world and who wrote, " life could not be endured were it seen in reality," it must sometimes have appeared to be a world suspended over an abyss.

II

WALTER SCOTT: THE WRITER

THE imperfections of a great writer are like the flaws in a precious stone: they should be regarded as qualities rather than faults. In Scott's case we have to take into account an attribute of the precious stone distinct from its quality or its rarity—its size. His mere bulk adds something spectacular and stupendous to him which his contemporaries felt and we can still feel. Where all is so huge, the faults are huge too; they are so obvious that certain critics have never been able to see beyond them. Mr. E. M. Forster, a man of genius and intelligence, has said that Scott is not even a good story-teller, and has demonstrated it by an amusing account of the plot of *The Antiquary*.

Scott was a very great story-teller, as well as a very bad one. *The Antiquary* certainly contains one of his worst plots. But his particular kind of story-telling did not depend on plot, and was often good in spite of it, the story being excellent even where the plot was mediocre or bad. A coherent plot obviously adds greatly to the total effect of a story, since all the incidents contribute to that effect. Such a story stays in the memory, not as a collection of episodes, but as a whole, and the cumulative movement of the action produces that emotional impression, the absence of which from Scott's poetry has been noted. This concentrated effect, which is like the effect of a whole mind directed on a single object, we find seldom in Scott's novels, and perhaps only in two—*The Heart of Midlothian*, his greatest story, and *The Bride of Lammermoor*, the story in which we have the strongest impression of fate.

But the coherent, necessitated plot is not his typical plot. His art as a story-teller could not have expanded to its full freedom within it, for with its emphasis on unity it did not give scope for the enormous degree of variety which he claimed. His stories in general have a direction; they set out from one point to reach another; but they take a rambling course, and there is nothing which they may not gather in before they reach their end. All the events in a story like *The Bride of Lammermoor* carry the mind forward to the conclusion. But in most of the Waverley Novels our minds are immediately fascinated by the succession of changing scenes which the journey produces, and the end is disappointing, being merely a conventional end. These stories consist mostly of middle; their abundance is all packed between the two conventions without which a story cannot exist, since it must start somehow and end somehow. The freedom which Scott demands from his plot, once he has started from somewhere to reach somewhere, is really a freedom to explore the whole human scene, and the laboured complication of the action is only a means to evoke a sense of the natural complications of human life. He is never tired of involving his plots, but he does so because he is endlessly interested in character and situation. And how brilliantly he manages it; his skill puts him among the greatest story-tellers.

The Fortunes of Nigel contains one of his most complicated plots. By any standard it is far too involved; the sequence of accidents to the papers securing young Lord Glenvarloch's possession of his estates becomes monstrous, absurd, almost wearisome. But what a variety of characters and scenes are gathered into the story by this stratagem, and what a liveliness is communicated to them by the vigour of the action. We must accept the complication of these plots as an artificial but necessary convention, as we accept the convention of the romantic opera.

In *The Fortunes of Nigel* Scott states a whole series of themes: the historical novelty of life in seventeenth-century London, the hostility between the English and the Scots whom the King had drawn south along with him, the connection with the mob through Vincent the apprentice, the connection with the Court through George Heriot. All this is stated in the first few chapters, and in the succeeding ones the fabric grows until it takes in the whole life of London. If Balzac had concentrated his powers to fill such a canvas, he would have done it in sections, devoting a separate book to each. Scott gathers the endless variety into one colossal whole. He does this without falling into confusion. The characters are thrown together pell-mell in the action; the classes intermingle in all sorts of ways; yet each figure remains as firmly in his station as the characters in the Prologue to *The Canterbury Tales*. Only a writer with Scott's fine sense of proportion could have been both so involved and so orderly. But the involution was necessary; it was the only means by which a novelist of action could have given an impression of the complication of human life.

The Fortunes of Nigel is Scott's most Baroque work. *Old Mortality* is comparatively simple in construction, because there he had a historical subject, the religious struggle in Scotland in the second half of the seventeenth century; the murder of Archbishop Sharpe and the battles of Drumclog and Bothwell Brig play an essential part in it. The action had to be woven round these important happenings. The invention is not free, therefore, as in *The Fortunes of Nigel*, being used to show in what ways the creed of the extreme Covenanters affected their character and speech, and above all to state dramatically the case of the two sides to the dispute. The opposing parties get entangled in personal relations with one another, as in *The Fortunes of Nigel*, their humanity prevailing over their opinions and loyalties. This happens in all the novels. Scott keeps two things evenly balanced in his scenes; his sense of universal humanity, and his awareness of the conventions of society. The first enables him to let people of all classes intermingle;

the second, to keep them intact in their places. No other novelist does this so surely. We may object to the philosophy of life implied by this performance, which is that of a traditional Tory; we may object to its being done at all; but we cannot but admire the perfection with which it is done. One might almost say that Scott puts man in his place, or rather what was once his place. And he does it so perfectly because he does it absent-mindedly.

In *Old Mortality* Scott needed all his objectivity, for he was dealing with an issue which was alive in his time and is not dead yet. Mr. Forster complains that Scott lacks both imaginative passion and artistic detachment. Actually Scott's detachment is sometimes disconcerting, is pushed to an extreme where we feel that nothing matters. It comes too easily; we feel he has no right to it. But in *Old Mortality* he had to make a hard effort to achieve detachment and state the case for both sides fairly, and this gives a tension to the action which is absent from most of the other novels.

But Scott's story-telling was, of course, mainly a device for delineating character. His most obvious virtue as a painter of character is the complexity of impression he achieves by apparently simple means. We are tempted to value lightly something which is achieved with such ease. We tend to think of his characters as simple characters; yet if we examine them we discover that hardly one is simple. Compared with those of Dickens or Fielding or Thackeray, they have infinite light and shade; though the light is so exactly where it should be, the shadow falls so naturally that we scarcely notice it. Yet they are all complex and surprising: Bailie Nicol Jarvie with his mixture of business sharpness and love of adventure; Andrew Fairservice with his cunning, conceit, self-righteousness and rustic poetry; and above all, James the Sixth of Scotland and First of England. Scott never tells us what James is thinking; he reveals him entirely through what he does and says. Yet he gives as completely as anyone could an impression of the bottomless complexity of that curious man, and leaves him a rounded character, a human being who successfully reconciles within himself outrageous irreconcilables. We cannot observe how it is done, the use of light and shade is so subtle, yet the figure so definite. Thackeray lavished all his skill on Becky Sharp, but she seems laboured and crude compared even with Scott's minor characters.

His supreme means for the revelation of character is, of course, dialogue; one feels sometimes that the action is contrived simply to give the characters an opportunity to speak out. And they put all of themselves into what they say, their dispositions, their moods, their memories, their philosophies. Scott knew that his main strength lay here, as he shows in an ironical imaginary dialogue between Dick Tinto, a painter, and himself at the beginning of *The Bride of Lammermoor*. " Your characters," Dick tells him, " make too much use of the *gob box*; they *patter* too much

... there is nothing in whole pages but mere chat and dialogue." The author replies: " The ancient philosopher was wont to say, ' Speak, that I may know thee '; and how is it possible for an author to introduce his *personæ dramatis* to his readers in a more interesting and effectual manner than by the dialogue in which each is represented as supporting his own appropriate character ? "

Scott's persons support their appropriate characters with unexampled eloquence, yet with the most exact proportion. Mr. Forster once remarked that the whole of Mrs. Micawber could be summed up in the sentence: " I shall never desert Mr. Micawber." Scott's characters cannot be contained in such formulas. They are not made up of one or two set qualities like the characters of Dickens; we feel that they are moulded from the substance of which human life is made, and contain all its attributes, the only difference between one character and another being that in them these attributes are compounded in different proportions. So that beyond the individual compounding there is something universally human which may burst out in some emergency, as in Jeanie Deans's appeal to the Queen.

In their light and shade, and in something unexpected in them, Scott's characters are unlike those of any other Scottish or English writer except some of Sterne's; for Sterne, too, was fascinated by the complexity of character. They are more like the characters of a novelist who in every other way was as unlike Scott as possible—Dostoevsky, particularly in the superb comic vein which he displays in the first part of *The Possessed*. Scott's characters have greater wholeness and harmony, and Dostoevsky's greater depth; but there is in both the same witty and acute contrast of qualities, the same paradoxicality, the same ability to be alive in a surprising way, as long as they are on the stage. Scott's grasp of the complexity of character came from his perception of human wholeness, and Dostoevsky's from his knowledge of man's inward division. But in their management of light and shade and a certain concealed or implied wit, they strikingly resemble each other.

Scott and Dostoevsky resemble each other in another way too, in their power to make their characters now and then say things of more than individual significance and turn them into voices which seem to speak for whole classes of humanity to all humanity. The only way to give an idea of these utterances is to quote some of them:

"I have had mony a thought, that when I faund mysell auld and forfairn, and no able to enjoy God's blessed air ony langer, I wad drag mysell here wi' a pickle aitmeal—and see, there's a bit bonny drapping well that popples that selfsame gate simmer and winter—and I wad e'en streek mysell out here, and abide my removal, like an auld dog that trails his useless ugsome carcase into some bush or bracken, no to gie living things a scunner wi' the sight o't when it's dead—Ay, and then, when the dogs barked at the lone farmstead, the gudewife wad cry, ' Whisht, stirra, that'll be auld Edie,' and the bits o' weans wad up, puir things, and toddle to the door, to pu' in the auld Blue Gown that mends a' their bonny-dies—but there wad be nae mair word o' Edie, I trow."

" I have been flitting every term these four and twenty years; but when the time comes there's aye something to saw that I would like to see sawn—or something to maw that I would like to see mawn—or something to ripe that I would like to see ripen—and sae I e'en daiker on wi' the family frae year's end to year's end. . . . But if your honour wad wush me ony place where I wad hear pure doctrine, and hae a free cow's grass, and a cot, and a yard, and mair than ten punds of annual fee, and where there was nae leddy about the town to count the apples, I'se hold mysell muckle indebted to ye."

" It's weel wi' you gentles, that can sit in the house wi' handkerchers at your een when ye lose a friend; but the likes o' us maun to our wark again if our hearts were beating as hard as my hammer. . . There's a curse either on me or on this auld black bitch of a boat that I have hauled up high and dry and patched and clouted sae mony years, that she might drown my poor Steenie at the end of them, an' be d—d to her! . . . Yet what needs ane be angry at her, that has neither soul nor sense? though I am no that muckle better mysell. She's but a rickle o' auld rotten deals . . . warped wi' the wind and the sea—and I am a dour carle, battered by foul weather at sea and land till I am maist as senseless as hersell. She maun be mended though again' the morning tide—that's a thing o' necessity."

" Do you see that blackit and broken end of a sheeling?—there my kettle boiled for forty years—there I bore twelve buirdly sons and daughters—where are they now?—where are the leaves that were on that auld ash-tree at Martinmas!—the west wind has made it bare—and I'm stripped too.—Do you see that saughtree?—it's but a blackened rotten stump now—I've sate under it mony a bonnie summer afternoon, when it hung its gay garlands ower the poppling water.—I've sat there and I've held you on my knee, Henry Bertram, and sung ye sangs of the auld barons and their bloody wars—It will ne'er be green again, and Meg Merrilies will never sing sangs mair, be they blithe or sad. But ye'll no forget her and ye'll gar big up the auld wa's for her sake?—and let somebody live there that's ower gude to fear them of another warld—For if ever the dead came back amang the living, I'll be seen in this glen mony a night after these crazed banes are in the mould."

In passages like these Scott speaks simultaneously from his daylight and his secret world.

G. M. YOUNG
1946

SCOTT AND THE HISTORIANS

WRITING of Gibbon and his early devotion to the *Arabian Nights*, I said : " The work of his manhood is shot with a child's visions of grave and bearded sultans who only smiled on the day of battle ; the sword of Alp Arslan, the mace of Mahmoud ; Imaus, and Caf, and Altai, and the Golden Mountains, and the Girdle of the Earth. To the Christian Middle Ages his imagination had no such key. No place in the world demands historic explanation so insistently as Venice. He passed through it with indifference and something like disgust. Gibbon's incomprehension of Mediaeval Europe is the measure of what history owes to Scott."

Among Scott's letters there is one dated 1806 and addressed to Lord Dalkeith, which, to the student of history and the writer of history, is of quite extraordinary interest, because Scott, without in the least realising that he was doing anything out of the common, has here furnished the social historian with an almost perfect example of method and presentation. The theme is the depopulation of the Southern Uplands between the Union of the Crowns and the middle of the eighteenth century, and there can hardly be one element, one operating cause, for which Scott has not allowed, to which he has not assigned due weight, in a letter only four or five pages long, but written with that full ease which gives the assurance of a vast reserve of knowledge behind every word. How had he come by it?

In his essay on Scott, written in 1858—that is, just a generation after Scott's death—Walter Bagehot let fall one highly suggestive observation. Grote, he said, had nowhere been more successful than in his attempt to derive from Homeric poetry a consistent account of Homeric society; and Scott's poetry is essentially a modernised version of the traditional poetry which his youth was spent in collecting. But such poetry, Bagehot goes on, is a sensible thing, dealing with incidents which have a form and a body and a prosaic consistence. He quotes from *The Lady of the Lake*:

> " Saxon, from yonder mountain high,
> I mark'd thee send delighted eye,
> Far to the south and east, where lay,
> Extended in succession gay,
> Deep waving fields and pastures green,
> With gentle slopes and groves between:
> These fertile plains, that soften'd vale,
> Were once the birthright of the Gael;
> The stranger came with iron hand,
> And from our fathers reft the land.
> Where dwell we now? See, rudely swell
> Crag over crag, and fell o'er fell.
> Ask we this savage hill we tread,
> For fatten'd steer or household bread;
> Ask we for flocks these shingles dry,
> And well the mountain might reply,—
> ' To you, as to your sires of yore,
> Belong the target and claymore!

> I give you shelter in my breast,
> Your own good blades must win the rest.'
>
> . . . . .
>
> Ay, by my soul! While on yon plain
> The Saxon rears one shock of grain,
>
> . . . . .
>
> The Gael, of plain and river heir,
> Shall, with strong hand, redeem his share."

And Bagehot comments that not in a set treatise could the relations of Highlander and Lowlander be more aptly described. But they are described, you see, in such words as come naturally to the lips of a man who thinks in terms of flocks and herds: the man, that is to say, who, in that letter to Lord Dalkeith, wrote the history of the depopulation in the language of people who remembered twenty chimneys smoking where now there were none, and who reckoned time from the waeful year when seven Scotts of the Forest lost their land.

It was from his own Border country and its traditions that Scott found his way into the past. As he says himself, " He that traverses these peaceful glens and hills *must* refer his researches to antiquity." Without antiquity, ruin and battlefield, the very line of demarcation

> Far in the distant Cheviots blue

are meaningless to the eye and say nothing to the imagination. With many minds this compulsion to make the place speak and tell its story seems to be a thing given by Nature, and so it was with Scott. I have sometimes tried to imagine him translated to England; that one year's sojourn in Bath prolonged to ten; and I have asked myself what shape his genius would have taken. He might, perhaps, have realised his whimsical ambition to be a dean! He would have published the Muniments of the Chapter House and restored the North Transept to his own design—and the subsequent fury of John Ruskin—and written one or two novels on the humours of life seen from the Cathedral Close, which might have been as interesting as *Columella* or *The Spiritual Quixote*—perhaps rather more. Because it is, I think, clear from *St. Ronan's Well* and the *Introduction to the Chronicles of the Canongate*, and above all from that exquisitely sympathetic piece, the humours of the Marquis de Vieuxbois, at the beginning of *Quentin Durward*, that Scott had it in him to be a novelist of contemporary life, to fill that rather puzzling gap between Fielding and Sterne on one side, and Dickens and Thackeray on the other, across which Miss Austen walks so daintily and so confidently on a path which is all her own. But the truth is, it is impossible to imagine Scott as anything but a Borderer, imbued from infancy with that sense of contrast, that feeling of something beyond, something mysteriously and magnetically different, which thrills us when Di Vernon points to Hawkesmoor Crag eighteen miles away, in Scotland, and Darcy Latimer walks by Solway and looks across the water, to England.

A French critic once distinguished the French from the English novel thus: that the French writer sets conventional characters in original situations, the English writer sets original characters in conventional situations. Well, with that oracular utterance in your mind read again the sixth chapter of *Rob Roy*. Here, besides the hero, who is also the narrator, you encounter three full-drawn characters, Rashleigh, Di Vernon and Andrew Fairservice; six adequately sketched in, Sir Hildebrand and his sons; with a tiny, but delightful, conversation-piece thrown in for good measure; old Martha, the housekeeper, having her sister's children to stay in the holidays and feeding them on berries from Andrew's garden. But go on. The hunting scenes which follow carry us to Inglewood Place and the old nonjuror who has taken the oaths for the common good, that is, for the enforcement of the Game Laws: and his clerk, Jobson, the Protestant zealot—with a passing glance at the Mayor of Newcastle who, for adequate reasons, was more partial to poachers than to sportsmen. Here in a very few pages Scott has given us a complete view of the conflict of Jacobite and Hanoverian as it was really felt in a Northumbrian Manor House in sight of Hawkesmoor Crag, eighteen miles from Scotland, over a range of characters, gross and subtle, fervent and apathetic, which covers the whole distance from Diana to Rashleigh. If it be complained that Scott might have given the Hanoverian cause a rather more stimulating representative than the amiable Francis, the answer is, first, that Francis is the hero, and Scott's heroes have nothing to do except to be amiable; and second, that of all causes for which men have fought and died, the Protestant succession as by law established was probably the least inspiring. It is characteristic of Scott that the only Hanoverian statesman he brings on the scene is a Highlander, a Campbell—the Duke of Argyll: and it is another Campbell " in a plain black dress with *couteau de chasse* "—who winds up the tale of the Stuarts and dismisses the exile in peace and for ever.

I am building up by instance and example my conception of Scott as the founder of a new and historic school, and here let me interpose one word of caution. We are so accustomed to regard Scott as the central figure in the Romantic Movement (if you think of it as a European movement I believe the word " central " is justified), and we are so accustomed to think of the Middle Ages as the Ages of Romance, that when you go over the list of Scott's writings you are surprised to notice how rarely he goes behind the Reformation, and one must add, with how little profit. Our positive knowledge, our popular knowledge, of the Middle Ages would have been no less if Scott had laid down his pen at the last page of *The Heart of Midlothian* and resumed it only to write *Redgauntlet*. *Ivanhoe* is one of the best stories ever written, but for all it has to tell us of England in the reign of Richard I it might be inscribed " Scene—a forest. Time—as you like it : " with a Saxon virago calling on Prussian deities in the idiom of Macpherson. Indeed, I am not sure that Scott did not give a lasting distortion to our conception of mediaeval history, by his fancy that Norman and Saxon persisted as consciously hostile races. From Scott, I suspect, came Thierry's notion that the cause of Becket was the cause of the Saxon against the Norman; and the even more remarkable belief of a French visitor, whose name I have forgotten, that in the England of 1840 no one was allowed to own a horse unless he could prove his Norman descent. That is not the only surviving fancy which the student of popular belief can trace to Scott. I once observed two commercial travellers contemplating the Abbey ruins from a window of the " Angel " at Bury St. Edmunds. " It is," said the more articulate of the two, " it is an interesting thought to think how many people were walled up alive in those old walls in ancient days." So much for Marmion.

But it is one of the most curious paradoxes of our literary history that the Middle Ages in England ceased to interest the educated intelligence just about the time when they began to lay hold on the educated fancy. For two generations or something more our mediaeval learning is a thing to wonder at. Hickes and Dugdale, Hearne and Wharton, Madox and Rymer really deserve to stand by the side of the great Benedictines, or the giants of the classical Renaissance. Then suddenly it all collapsed under the weight of rational disdain. The tide which had borne these splendid argosies of learning, the Monasticon and the Foedera, turned and ran backwards, leaving the vessels aground and their freights undischarged. But simultaneously the Middle

Ages became romantic, and from this unblessed union of ignorance and fascination came, in due course, Strawberry Hill, *The Castle of Otranto*, Ossian, Mrs. Radcliffe, and, with sorrow we must add, *Count Robert of Paris* and the Vehmgericht in *Anne of Geierstein*. But, when the revival came, the whole educated world was, as we might say, conditioned to read its documents as Scott would have read them and so to see the mediaeval world, not as a pageant, but as a social structure where all, high or low, are linked together by the same customary law. So it came about that Bagehot's saying might be inverted: not in a work of fiction now do we expect such vivid pictures of social relations as we find in historical treatises, in Maitland's *Domesday and Beyond*, in the prefaces to the successive volumes of the Selden Society, or in those books whose names will always be a renewal of grief to all who remember Eileen Power.

Let me give an example from those fascinating vignettes of old English life, the *Inquests in Proof of Age*. Martin the Miller aged 60 years or upwards avers that he was crossing the churchyard on the Vigil of St. Oswald, in the third year of our Lord the King that now is, and he saw a christening party and they told him it was Henry's son. John atte Townsend says that Henry's daughter Catherine came running out of her chamber to tell him she had a brother for which she gave thanks to God. William Weaver was hunting the fox that day with Henry, when a man ran up and said, " Sir, will you hear the news?" and he said, "Fair friend, what news?" and the man said, "Sir, there is a son born in your house," and Henry gave him forty pence. Asked by the court how he comes to remember the date so well, he says his cousin was married that morning, and after the wedding there was a feast, and after the feast there was a fray, and "I was fined sixpence in the King's court for breaking my fellow's head." Well, that is the Middle Ages. It is a world where everybody is, we may say, interested in everybody else, and may be required to declare his interest; everybody knows something about everybody else and may be required to divulge his knowledge.

To show Scott's originality and mastery in this field, take a passage from one of his poorest works, *The Monastery*, where he is describing the state of the church tenants on the eve of the Reformation. He dwells on the superior skill of those protected holders of monastic land, and, though doubtless in humble measure, their greater wealth. They are better informed, better fed, more independent, than their neighbours. From the kindly monks the boy of talent might get some learning, while the fathers of the hamlet, having more time for reflection as well as stronger motives for improving their properties, bore amongst their neighbours the character of shrewd, intelligent men who dreaded nothing more than to be involved in the feuds of secular landlords.

Now here you have, it seems to me, a new type coming into existence, the result of certain peculiar circumstances which could only exist in a border county remote from the control of the Crown. Pacific but not untrained in arms ; not to be trodden on with impunity ; acquainted with book learning but skilful in husbandry, hard living but comfortable, independent and not without a pleasing sense of their own superiority to their neighbours. And thus, or somehow thus, I think, is how the commons of Scotland do present themselves to a southern eye. They are not a yeomanry, open-handed and careless ; they are a true peasantry, and one which, we all know, has exercised a profound influence on our civilisation throughout the world.

Now, to the historian the development of types like that is always a matter of great interest. In England the Reformation created a gentry. In Scotland it created a peasantry. Why ? Well, Scott, it seems to me, has in these pages gone far to give an answer—whether it is the right answer I do not know, and I do not think it very much matters. What does matter is that he has gone the right way to find it—by tracing causes back until you find yourself among the good folk of Kennaquhair, and learn what you could never have guessed yourself—that while it was a venial sin to borrow one of the King's good deer, a heavy penance followed the sin of " start and overloup," that is, of following the moss-troopers on a foray to Cumberland, and so inviting reprisals on the lands of St. Mary. Now of " start and overloup " we in the south knew nothing. We were much too well-governed, much too frequently and impartially hanged. The lack of historic memory has often been noticed as an English characteristic. But generations of firm government had left us with nothing to remember. You know how in *Woodstock* and *Peveril* Scott labours to make something happen, and what a poor business it all ends in. He was writing of a country where nothing ever did happen; the police saw to that. Feuds that in Scotland would have decimated the countryside were here brought promptly to a stop by the tything man, white rod in hand, telling the parties to go home and behave, or they would find themselves in the Star Chamber.

Now was that the reason why, when the commons of Scotland crossed the Tweed in defence of the Covenant, the commons of England, to put it mildly, had one good look at them and decided to go home, while the House of Lords hurriedly passed a sessional order that the newcomers should henceforth be referred to as " our brethren " (not as hitherto, " those lousy Scots ")? Well, it may be so. I leave it to the historians to discover.

I have just let slip once or twice the word " romantic." You know what a dangerous lure that word is to those of us who concern ourselves with the history of opinion, of feeling, or of taste. And no one can ever pronounce it without recalling the exquisite scholarship which Logan Pearsall-Smith devoted to its history. You remember the line of descent as he established it. First of all it means " like the fables of chivalry in *lingua romanica* or their later imitations." Then, by a swift turn, " like the landscape of such stories." To Aubrey and Evelyn Salisbury Plain is romantic, partly because there are shepherdesses there, and partly because old men had seen Philip Sidney riding in Vernditch chase, and sometimes reining in his horse to capture and write down some new felicity for his *Arcadia*. To Pope Windsor is " the most romantic castle " in the world. And Addison, viewing the place of the Magdalen's penance amongst the rocks and mountains of Southern France, writes, " It is so romantic a scene that it has almost probably given occasion to such chimerical relations." That is the eighteenth century, the century of reason bidding its little pupils not to be fanciful, and, of course, Addison was a Whig. Did you notice an echo from the Western Islands ? Johnson was a Tory. " Far from me and my friends be such frigid philosophy as may conduct us indifferent and unmoved over any ground which has been dignified by wisdom, bravery or virtue. That man is little to be envied whose patriotism would not gain force upon the plain of Marathon or whose piety would not grow warmer among the ruins of Iona." Between Addison and Johnson the conception, as it were, had taken charge of itself ; it was beginning to spread its glamour over sea and land ; and, gathering up the sentiment which such scenes were now permitted to evoke, it returned to literature, enriching and enriched.

I must not linger even on the outskirts of this illimitable theme. But I should like to point out that romance, being in its origin a local sentiment, gave a new significance to place, to the scene of action, and it was Scott who first applied the incoming craft of local description to the composition of history. To the new school the question, " Where did it happen ? " would be quite as important as, " How did it happen ? " Indeed the two are hardly to be separated. And in his narrative of Drumclog and the victory of the Covenanters over the King's Guards, Scott set an example and a standard which some of his successors, professed historians, may have reached, but none, I think, has ever surpassed. And not the scene only but, to use a word which was coming into fashion when Scott was a boy, the scenery of action can now be transferred to the canvas. Macaulay was far too Augustan to share the annual raptures of clerks and milliners at Loch Katrine and Loch Lomond, but he cannot help himself. At Killiecrankie he must write about " the sound, so musical to modern ears, of the river falling down the mossy rocks and amongst smooth pebbles, the masses of grey crag and dark verdure worthy of the pencil of Wilson, the fantastic peaks bathed at sunrise and sunset with light as rich as that which glows on the canvas of Claude."

Now where does that come from ? Well, I think the seed was lodged in the most capacious memory ever given to mortal man by Julia Mannering, because this is how she writes of Cumberland to her " dearest Matilda " in that letter where, in passing, I think you first encounter that genius for friendship without which no obituary is complete. She writes: " If India be the land of magic ... this is the country of romance. The scenery is such as nature brings together in her sublimest moods; sounding cataracts—hills which rear their scathed heads to the sky—lakes that, winding up the shadowy valleys, lead at every turn to yet more romantic recesses—rocks which catch the clouds of heaven. All the wildness of Salvator here, and there the fairy scenes of Claude." Macaulay writes better than Julia Mannering, I grant you, but the staple of both passages, you see, is the same—that early romantic picturesque which Scott, who learned it from Mrs. Radcliffe, wove into the texture of history.

Scott, you remember, was mature in years when he embarked on this business of romantic fiction. He did not need to search for incident or character, he had only to dip and draw, and those raids into Liddesdale, year after year repeated, had furnished him with a good store of both. But compare him with Dickens. You feel, I think, that with Scott observation and invention are under a certain control, the control of a mind trained to disengage the relevant from the incidental and the essential from the local: to weigh testimonies, to balance probabilities, to estimate the force of motives among all sorts and conditions of men. In a word it is the mind of a lawyer, a lawyer interested not so much in the higher branches of his science as in the human spectacle which is for ever unrolling before the lawyer's eye, and which it is the business of the lawyer to reduce to order.

But would those two things—the equipment and the discipline—be enough to account for the Waverley Novels? Hardly. We need some impulse, some crystallising touch, and we know whose fingers gave it. Scott—we have his own avowal—set out to do for Scotland what Maria Edgeworth had done for Ireland. And what had she done? She had painted a picture, not of contemporary Ireland, but of an Ireland just fading on the view, about as far from her eye as the '45 was from Scott, not quite so far as Trollope is from us. Of course, it was impossible to confine an epic genius like Scott's within the elegant frame which Maria Edgeworth just filled. None the less it is worth while reading one of the early Waverley Novels like *Rob Roy* or *The Antiquary* with an eye for the Edgeworth strain in the fabric. You catch it in the garden at Osbaldistone Hall. You hear a very familiar strain in the protestations of Mrs. Macleuchar, who keeps the " laigh shop," *anglice*, a cellar, opening on to the High Street. And in passages like these you realise that Miss Edgeworth had given him the one thing which was really indispensable for the development of his power, and that was the example of an idiom. It is, as I think Saintsbury once said, the idiom that gives her stories their amazing verisimilitude. Sir Patrick's funeral is enough. " All the gentlemen of the three counties were at it, far and near how they flocked; my great grandfather said that, to see all the women in their red cloaks you would have taken them for the Army drawn out. Then such a fine willaluh! you might have heard it to the farthest end of the county, and happy the man who could get but a sight of the hearse."

She has, you see, faced and overcome what is one of the greatest difficulties of fiction, I mean the difficulty of making the characters really talk. And her example released, one might say, Scott's gift for language. He had already at his command a full keyboard of dialect, from the illustrious and courtly vernacular, such as old ladies who had danced at Holyrood with the Chevalier, still spoke, to the hardly human lingo of the Dougal creature in the Tolbooth at Glasgow, and in Scott's hand every one of them rings true. He had thought a great deal about this question of language. He knew his Defoe, he confesses that the incomparable conversation between Bothwell and old Milnwood in *Old Mortality* was lifted straight from Defoe's *History of the Union*. And for his own purposes Defoe's dialect is perfect. In what other language could he have written the *Journal of the Plague*? But then, Defoe makes Gustavus Adolphus talk exactly like a stevedore by London Bridge. Scott wanted something better, and left to himself he could not find it. In his essay on Clara Reeve he sets out his difficulties and his solution.

To interest a modern reader, he says, the writer must invest his characters with a language unknown to their time, a compromise like the apparel of King Lear, who wears neither the robes of King George nor the blue paint of an ancient Briton. And Scott, in effect, recommends a factitious antique, the style of our grandfathers and great-grandfathers, sufficiently out of date to correspond with the time of the story, and sufficiently copious for the characters to express sentiments which they never felt.

That is really not very promising, and the result, as we all know, is that if Richard and Wilfred talk like our great-grandfathers, Gurth and Wamba talk like nothing on earth. It is unsafe to trust one's memory for the contents of forty-eight volumes, but I cannot recall one passage where Scott is genuinely humorous in English and only one where he is truly eloquent—the judgment given in the case of "The Two Drovers," which is indeed one of the noblest passages in English fiction. And the clumsy Late-Augustan which furnishes the staple of his dialogue is a language only fit for Scott's heroes to make love in to Scott's heroines. Sometimes it seems designed for even lowlier purposes. " Circumstances have been communicated to us of a nature so extraordinary that, reluctant as I am to exercise such authority . . . I am constrained to request from you an explanation of them." To my ear, that sentence from *The Monastery* suggests that the Ministry of Agriculture and Fisheries is getting really cross with the Ministry of Fuel and Power.

But whenever Scott is speaking in dialect, a magical reality comes over the scene. Suppose, I have sometimes thought, that I had *Ivanhoe* and *Kenilworth* and *Woodstock* to go on, and an anonymous manuscript was brought to me. Should I have guessed that the author of the printed books had it in him to conceive the outpourings of David Deans, to tell the tale of Wandering Willie's grandsire, or to write that magnificent descant in *Guy Mannering*: " Ride your ways, Laird of Ellangowan—ride your ways, Godfrey Bertram." I doubt it. They belong to a different kind of mind.

Now, I have dwelt on that because of its bearing on what I hope you will not think me too bold in calling the revolution effected by Scott in the writing of history, and particularly of mediaeval history. The secret is to treat every document as the record of a conversation, and go on reading till you hear the people speaking. And that is, or will be, the keyword of the new school. " What happened here? " the older generation might ask. " No battle was fought, no treaty was signed, no council assembled —pass on." Their successors will answer, " People were talking. Let us stop and listen." " It was never right nor justice, double doom to take for one trespass." Well, that is the case of Becket against the Crown. But where was that judgment given? In King's Bench? It sounds much more like the King's Arms. But that, I repeat, is the Middle Ages. That is how the history of institutions must be written, being the record at once of what happened, and what people said about it when it was happening.

Now, Scott himself never knew what treasures of record were lying just below the surface. But he did show those who came after him how to handle the lore which the great scholars of the mediaeval revival disclosed : how to search for historic truth impartially and unconstrainedly on the battlefield and in the sheepfold, in court and cottage and counting-house, knowing that the object of history is nothing less than the setting forth of an entire culture. You can see this new idea pushing to the front in Voltaire, in Robertson, even in Johnson's *Hebrides*, but it was Scott who put the conception into currency; not by any express doctrine, but by the enchantment of his practice; not of set purpose but by the instinctive movement of a mind equipped and constituted as we have seen, the mind of a Borderer who was also a lawyer. I need not remind you how large a place—some readers find it too large—the law and its humours occupy in Scott's pages, but I should like to point out how the discipline, the legal discipline, operates in shaping that masterpiece of character and contrast, " The Two Drovers " : the wonderful economy with which the narrative is managed, how we are told all we need to know and no more ; and how we are compelled to hold our judgment until the tale is completed. Only a lawyer could have written that, and among lawyers, I think, only one who, like his own Counsellor Pleydell, had listened to the tale of the hill folk in their own speech and had himself perambulated the marches of Lewinshope and Broadmeadow, below Penmenscaur.

Let us take another example of Scott's craftsmanship in the field he opened to the historians of the next age—the twelfth chapter of the *Bride of Lammermoor* and the breakdown of feudal economy at Wolf's-hope. Observe the elements as Scott puts them in their place. Hereditary respect for the lord—that still survives. But the tenants have prudently contrived to get parchments, title deeds to their little holdings, and so broken the chain of feudal dependence without as yet acquiring any sense, or habit, of freedom. That came later: first they grumbled, then they resisted, finally they refused to comply. In vain did Caleb point out that, as a matter of understanding, Ravenswood was entitled to his Monday egg. They scratched their heads and answered " They could not say." At length the cooper rose and said the hens had cackled many a day for Ravenswood, and it was time they cackled for those that gave them roost and barley. He proposes to call in the law in the person of Davie Dingwall, and Davie arrives, his portmanteau stuffed with feu-charters, and behind Davie all the powers of the Crown embodied in a Corporal and four redcoats. Which word in passing starts another hare. A redcoat is an English soldier, more especially a soldier of the Parliamentary army. Has Scott made a slip, or did the statesmen of the Revolution time find it convenient to employ English soldiers on these necessary but disagreeable duties? However that may be, Scott has, so to speak, taken one drop out of the stream of history, and shown us as in a microscope what this transformation, the passage from status to contract, really meant to those who lived through it, and by their words and doings brought it about. Here indeed we have, in Maitland's words, men's common thought of common things.

A little while back I used the word "contrast." May I remind you that among educated speakers in Scott's time it had not altogether shed its technical and pictorial meaning: the balancing of figures in opposition, the assembly of carefully graduated distances. Well on in the nineteenth century we find Emerson writing: "The steep contrasts of condition make the picturesque in society." Now, if you take three great masters of observation, Chaucer, Shakespeare and Scott, you will notice how much more naturally and easily Chaucer and Scott take these contrasts than Shakespeare does. Think of the Pilgrims. "What a crowd," you may say; "how uncomfortable they must have been in each other's company." They are not a crowd, they are a fellowship, and knowing their place they know exactly how to behave.

> " Wel seyd, by corpus dominus," quod our hoste,
> " Now longe moot thou sayle by the coste,
> Sir gentil maister, gentil marineer!
> God yeve this monk a thousand last quad yeer!
> But now passe over, and lat us seke aboute,
> Who shal now telle first, of al this route,
> Another tale;" and with that word he sayde,
> As curteisly as it had been a mayde,
> " My lady Prioresse, by your leve,
> So that I wiste, I sholde yow nat greve,
> I wolde demen that ye tellen sholde
> A tale next, if so were that ye wolde.
> Now wol ye vouche-sauf, my lady dere?"
> " Gladly," quod she, and seyde as ye shal here.

Now, Walter Raleigh, I remember, somewhere said that Shakespeare never quite knew what to do with his working classes. He can make them gloriously funny and at times extremely tiresome, and when they are not losing themselves in the thickets of learned speech they are spouting morality, like the oldest inhabitant accounting for his longevity to our special correspondent.

> Though I am old yet I am strong and lusty
> For in my youth I never did apply
> Hot and rebellious liquors to my blood.

This theatrical convention comes down, I suppose, from the mischievous slaves and pedagogues of ancient comedy. But for the most part, the world would get on just as well if no such people existed. Until we come to *The Winter's Tale.* And in the sheep-shearing which is the nodus of the plot you remember how evenly the comedy and poetry is distributed, how necessary the Shepherd and Clown, even Autolycus, are to the conduct of the fable; how easily they all sustain their parts, with what aptness they all speak. They are comic, broadly comic—but they are not comic relief. The play could not get on without them, nor could the world. Shakespeare has discovered that. Chaucer and Scott always knew it. The fate of the Empire turns on the bonds which Mr. Owen travelled to Glasgow to recover, and poor Peter Peebles has his part to play in the last sad hour of the House of Stuart. A convention has been swept away, the canvas of historic fiction has been enlarged. We may forget that what, as much as anything else, took Europe by storm was the abundance and variety and reality of Scott's characters. And when once the canvas of fiction had been enlarged the canvas of history could be enlarged too.

Antiquary, poet and novelist as he was, Scott, we are never likely to forget, was a man immersed in the daily life of his own time. And how did he conceive the transition, the convulsion through which his own world was passing? The *Life of Napoleon* happens to be a favourite bedside book of mine, and as I only read it as a prelude to sleep I am hardly qualified to appreciate it critically. Goethe, if I remember right, took the precaution, not unknown to less eminent practitioners, of reviewing it before he read it, and he assured a French visitor that it was inaccurate and partial. But he laid his finger on the essential truth when he said that it is a document for the history of England. Often, as I read it drowsily, the fancy comes over me that I am not reading but listening—that supper is over, the cups are filled and the minstrel has been sent for to tell once more how the false Frenchman forsook his faith and, giving himself over to the powers of evil, was smitten again and again by sea and land until the world had peace. I do not wonder it made Sainte-Beuve or any Frenchman dance with rage. And Sainte-Beuve selects for special censure the abundance of metaphor and simile which, if you come to think of it, are essential to the fullness of the epic style. In fact,

I have sometimes found myself dreamily turning these flowers of narrative into similes after the Homeric manner. " As when children playing together make a little hut of boughs and branches, hoping that their elder kinsfolk will take refuge in it, but they pass by unnoticing, or even tread it underfoot, even so did the Girondins think that they had planned a constitution." The parallel seems to me to be brilliantly illuminating, and almost disquietingly applicable to others besides the Girondins!

Certainly the *Life of Napoleon* adds no more to the fame of Scott than the " Ode on the Peace " adds to the fame of Wordsworth. But there are two sorts of historical themes, the logical and the psychological. One, having set its zero hour, undertakes to show how and why things happened as they did, and the other what did it feel like to be alive when they were happening. Now, Scott felt like a loyal subject to King George and a Tory, one of those who knew that the Corsican could be beaten, when the faint-hearted Whigs were proving that he could not, and who all the time could not convince themselves that even Mr. Pitt, and still less Mr. Perceval, were going the right way about it. Stubborn, anxious, proud, often bewildered but never dismayed. I find the picture true. I think that is the spirit which wore Napoleon down, the spirit which, even in the heat of battle or the more bitter conflicts of party, never quite forgot what was due to the other side. And Scott, the passionate political partisan, shows,

I think, a more thorough understanding of the English radicals who opposed the war than Macaulay shows of the English Jacobites, or Froude of the English Catholics.

But to our question : how did Scott feel ? how did he conceive the transition of which he was the witness? It is a question always worth asking about a historian, because the historian is one to whom the past has something of the homely triviality of the present, and the present already has some thing of the shadowy magnificence of the past. I think the answer is given in his letter to Joanna Baillie about the new railroad. " Half proud, half angry, half sad and half pleased." It is typical of Scott, with his intensely practical mind, that he should have foreseen the changes the railway would effect years before they elicited from the Duke of Wellington his magisterial pronouncement, " I see no reason to suppose that these machines will ever force themselves into general use," and Doctor Arnold's later judgment, " Railways have given the death blow to feudalism." It was impossible not to be pleased, impossible not to be proud of the great industrial achievement of the age. And yet what was the price to be paid ? To Wordsworth, in the last Books of *The Excursion*, the loss of individual human dignity. To Scott, the break-up of a social order which, one might say, he had kept alive by main force of his imagination. The new industrialism, blending with old revolutionary discontent, was creating that radicalism which overshadowed Scott's later years and found voice in the cry, "Burke Sir Walter!" from his own Border people. It is Wolf's-hope once more. It is the severing of those stable and friendly relations which to Scott were the living tissue of a healthy stock.

It was, I think, his deep and simple conviction that if the relations between the Duke of Buccleuch and Walter Scott, and between Walter Scott and Tom Purdie, had existed in France there would have been no French Revolution because there would have been no need for one. Now they were snapping everywhere. And in one part of the kingdom, in his own country, in those Highlands which he had made famous and as familiar to the world as Homer's Ithaca and Homer's Troy, that future was not only dark but desolate. Clanship was no more; and the passage in which Scott recounts its end is one of the most moving, and, in its eloquence, one of the truest things ever written in history, the kind of history which Scott taught the next generation to read, to write and to understand.

A milder race arose;—the Highlanders with whom our youth was conversant, cultivating sedulously the means of subsistence which their country afforded, and converting the broadsword into the ploughshare, and the spear into the herdsman's crook, yet preserving an aptitude to military habits, and an enthusiastic energy of character derived from the recollections of former days, and fostered by the tales of the grey-headed veterans, who looked back with regret to the days when each man's arms clattered round him when he walked the hills. Among these men, the spirit of clanship subsisted no longer indeed as a law of violence, but still as a law of love. They maintained, in many instances, their chiefs at their own expense; and they embodied themselves in regiments, that the head of the family might obtain military preferment. . . Some such distinction between Highlanders and Lowlanders . . . would long have subsisted, had it been fostered by those who, we think, were most interested in maintaining it. The dawn of civilisation would have risen slowly on the system of Highland Society; and as the darker and harsher shades were already dispelled, the romantic contrast and variety reflected upon ancient and patriarchal usages, by the general diffusion of knowledge, would, like the brilliant colours of the morning clouds, have survived for some time, ere blended with the general mass of ordinary manners. In many instances, Highland proprietors have laboured with laudable and humane precaution to render the change introduced by a new mode of cultivation gentle and gradual, and to provide, as far as possible, employment and protection for those families who were thereby dispossessed of their ancient habitations. But in other, and in but too many instances, the glens of the Highlands have been drained, not of their superfluity of population, but of the whole mass of the inhabitants, dispossessed by an unrelenting avarice, which will be one day found to have been as short-sighted as it is unjust and selfish. Meanwhile, the Highlands may become the fairy ground for romance and poetry, or subject of experiment for the professors of speculation, political and economical.—But if the hour of need should come—and it may not, perhaps, be far distant—the pibroch may sound through the deserted region, but the summons will remain unanswered. The children who have left her will re-echo from a distant shore the sounds with which they took leave of their own—*Ha til, ha til, ha til, mi tulidh!*—" We return—we return—we return—no more!"

S. C. ROBERTS
1948

Reprinted from
The University of Edinburgh Journal, 1948
Vol. XIV, No. 3

I
THE MAKING OF A NOVELIST

For a lecturer to begin with an apology is fatal. But I may perhaps be permitted to say an introductory word about the peculiar circumstances which led to my appointment as the Scott Lecturer for this present year. When I was honoured with the invitation in the first instance, I endeavoured to be honest in my reply: I was honest in saying how much I was attracted by the prospect of renewing my relations with an Edinburgh audience; I was equally honest, I hope, in stating my lamentable lack of qualification for the task. I will not here repeat verbatim the somewhat colloquial retort which I received from your Professor, but the gist of it was that after having listened to expositions by professional scholars on various aspects of Scott's life and work, the audience might perhaps be entertained by the impressions of an unjustified beginner.

In such a situation I may perhaps take comfort, and at the same time take warning, from Scott himself. In his autobiographical fragment he writes:

> Feeling myself greatly inferior to my companions in metaphysical philosophy and other branches of regular study, I laboured, not without some success, to acquire at least such a portion of knowledge as might

enable me to maintain my rank in conversation. In this I succeeded pretty well; but unfortunately then, as often since through my life, I incurred the deserved ridicule of my friends from the superficial nature of my acquisitions, which being, in the mercantile phrase, *got up* for society, very often proved flimsy in the texture. . . .

How refreshing is the candour of that paragraph and indeed of the whole of the *Autobiography* and how different from the dreary records of precocity which frequently characterise the early pages of literary biography—Pope plunging into miscellaneous reading at the age of twelve so eagerly that his feeble constitution threatened to break down, and when about seventeen he despaired of recovery and wrote a farewell to his friends; Milton, of whom it was written, " When he was very young he studied very hard and sate up very late, commonly till 12 or 1 o'clock at night; and his father ordered the maid to sit up for him "; John Stuart Mill, who from his eighth to his twelfth year read " the Bucolics and six books of the Æneid of Vergil, five books of Livy, all Sallust, parts of Ovid, Terence and Lucretius, several of Cicero's Orations and the Letters to Atticus, the Iliad and Odyssey, all Thucydides, the Hellenics of Xenophon, a great part of the Attic orators, Theocritus, Anacreon, several books of Polybius and, lastly, Aristotle's Rhetoric." From such devastating priggishness Scott's early years were happily free. From the beginning, reading was for him a recreation; just as his writing was ultimately to be recreation in the fullest and most literal sense of the word. As a boy, his lameness determined that he should have more than the normal amount of leisure, and some of it was spent in reading Pope's Homer aloud to his mother. At school he liked to try his hand at poetical versions of Vergil and Horace, and one of the first poets that won his enthusiasm was Spenser, not because he was the poet's poet, but because he told a tale of chivalry: " Too young to trouble myself about the allegory, I considered all the knights and ladies and dragons and giants in their outward and exoteric sense, and God only knows how delighted I was to find myself in such society."

But the climax of delight came at the age of thirteen, when beneath a platanus tree he read on and on, forgetting the dinner-hour, entranced in the intellectual banquet afforded by Bishop Percy's *Reliques of Ancient Poetry.* " To read and to remember," he said, " was in this instance the same thing." From that moment he began to devour all that was adventurous and romantic.

Having introduced that dangerous key-word, I feel impelled to embark upon some measure of definition. Heaven forbid that I should attempt to add yet another chapter to the swollen bibliography of the subject. But when we glibly refer to Scott as one of the greatest of the Romantics, or as the man who primarily inspired the Romantic movement in France, it is well to determine what we mean. " Romanticism," wrote Professor Butterfield in an early essay on the historical novel, " is at bottom a sigh for the things that perish and the things that can never happen again." Now that is a definition which is clearly inapplicable to Scott. Scott greeted the pageant of past history not with a wistful sigh, but with a shout of exultation; give him a pen in his hand and he would make the events happen again in a couple of months. Furthermore, the conception of Romance as simply a meditation upon the picturesque glories of past ages is but a part of the story. If we are confronted with the question, " What is the most revealing example of a truly ' romantic ' poem ? " I suppose that most of us would point to " The Ancient Mariner " or, still better, to " La Belle Dame sans Merci " :

> O what can ail thee, knight-at-arms,
>   Alone and palely loitering ?
> The sedge is withered from the lake,
>   And no birds sing.

Here there is something more than a love of mediaeval knight-errantry. There is mystery, there is a magic hush in those last dragging monosyllables; we are on the threshold of something not comprehensible in terms of ordinary experience, we are at the portals of faery lands forlorn. The poem is a sigh not for the things that can never happen again, but for the things that never have happened at all. Behind it and inspiring it is a metaphysical search for absolute Truth and Beauty.

Now Scott, as we have seen, did not lay claim to any deep interest in metaphysical enquiry.

Old ballads, old battle-scenes, old buildings, old mountain-ranges roused in him immediate enthusiasm, but it was the enthusiasm of the story-teller, not the vision of the romantic seer. His feeling for the beauties of natural objects was, he says, awakened at quite an early age:

> The romantic feelings which I have described as predominating in my mind, naturally rested upon and associated themselves with these grand features of the landscape around me; and the historical incidents, or traditional legends connected with many of them, gave to my admiration a sort of intense impression of reverence, which at times made my heart feel too big for its bosom. From this time the love of natural beauty, more especially when combined with ancient ruins, or remains of our fathers' piety or splendour, became with me an insatiable passion.

This is admirably clear and characteristic; natural beauty roused his admiration, but what made his heart beat faster was the historical incident or traditional legend associated with it. One comment on some of his earliest poetic writing was: " Upon my word, Walter Scott is going to turn out a poet—something of a cross, I think, between Burns and Gray "; and a certain affinity between Scott and the fastidious recluse of my own College has more than once been noted.

> Right against the eastern gate,
> By the moss-grown pile he sate;
> Where long of yore to sleep was laid
> The dust of the prophetic Maid.
> Facing to the northern clime,
> Thrice he traced the runic rhyme;

> Thrice pronounc'd, in accents dread,
> The thrilling verse that wakes the Dead:
> Till from out the hollow ground
> Slowly breathed a sullen sound.

These are lines from Gray's *The Descent of Odin*, but I conjecture that they might deceive all but the elect.

In a certain sense, indeed, Gray may be claimed as more strictly romantic than Scott. Writing from Turin in 1739 to his friend West, Gray gives some impressions of his continental tour in a famous letter:

> I own I have not, as yet, anywhere met with those grand and simple works of Art, that are to amaze one, and whose sight one is to be the better for: But those of Nature have astonished me beyond expression. In our little journey up to the Grande Chartreuse, I do not remember to have gone ten paces without an exclamation, that there was no restraining. Not a precipice, not a torrent, not a cliff, but is pregnant with religion and poetry. There are certain scenes that would awe an atheist into belief, without the help of other argument.

Now Scott had his own view of atheists. "There are few, I trust," he wrote in his Journal, "who disbelieve the existence of a God; nay, I doubt if at all times, and in all moods, any single individual ever adopted that hideous creed, though some have professed it. With the belief of a Deity, that of the immortality of the soul and of the state of future rewards and punishments is indissolubly linked. More we are not to know. . . ."

Scott's religious belief, indeed, was firmly based; but its foundation was ethical and social, rather than theological. "I would, if called upon, die a martyr for the Christian religion," he wrote, "so completely is (in my opinion) its divine origin proved by its beneficial effects on the state of society"; and when poor Mr. Huntly Gordon could not face the trials of ordination, Scott replied: "Leave this matter to me—do you work away at the Catalogue, and I'll write for you a couple of sermons that shall pass muster well enough at Aberdeen." The two discourses which resulted, one on "The Christian and the Jewish Dispensations Compared" and the other on "The Blessedness of the Righteous," are admirable examples of Scott's approach to Scriptural problems.

When Scott first visited Iona in 1810, he wrote to Miss Joanna Baillie: "From this rude and remote island the light of Christianity shone forth on Scotland and Ireland. The ruins are of a rude architecture, but curious to the Antiquary." Inevitably we miss the fervour of Johnson's famous outburst: "That man is little to be envied whose patriotism would not gain force upon the plain of Marathon or whose piety would not grow warmer among the ruins of Iona." It is but fair to add that when Scott revisited the island on his tour of the lighthouses, he recorded his impressions at much greater length and noted the aptness of Erskine's allusion, in the reading of prayers, to the ship's company being in sight of " the first Christian Church from which

Revelation was diffused over Scotland and all its islands"; but Scott's immediate and instinctive feeling is summed up in his quotation of the lines:
> You never tread upon them but you set
> Your feet upon some ancient history.

Such are the perils of digression provoked by the most modest attempt to examine the word " romantic." One thing at least is clear. The revelation that came to Scott through the medium of old Border ballads and other ancient poems was in no sense a mystical revelation. The mediaeval legends might well contain elements of mystery and magic, and Scott seized upon such elements with a boyish delight which persisted throughout his life; but he continued to regard them in their " outward and exoteric " sense; with the mystery of the Universe he was not concerned. " How," asks Hippolyte Taine, " could the great Catholic and mystical dreams . . . find entrance into the head of this gentlemanly citizen ? "

With the poems in Bishop Percy's collection remembered as soon as read and recited as soon as remembered, it was but natural that Scott should himself become a writer as well as a collector of ballad-poetry. At the age of twenty-five he indulged his own vanity by publishing translations of two ballads by Bürger, but more important was the *Minstrelsy of the Scottish Border* (1802), a collection which included a number of his own pieces, such as " The Eve of Saint John " and " The Gray Brother." With this book Scott enjoyed what he calls " the first gleam of public favour," although it was "one of those books which are more praised than they are read"—an extensive category, though few authors are as clear-sighted as Scott in recognising that their own books may belong to it.

Scott's passionate study of ballad-literature bore its first ripened fruit in *The Lay of the Last Minstrel*. Published in 1805, it achieved a sale commensurate with its general approbation. " In the history of British Poetry," wrote Lockhart, "nothing had ever equalled the demand for The Lay of the Last Minstrel." Scott, as always, was entirely frank about the casual inception and development of the poem. The beautiful Lady Dalkeith had been told a legend of a Dwarf Page and asked Scott to make a ballad out of it. So lovely and irresistible was the lady that Scott was bound to assent—if she had asked for a ballad on a broomstick he would have had to make the attempt. So a few verses, to be entitled " The Goblin Page," were begun. His friend Sir John Stoddart had recited to him Coleridge's unfinished and unpublished " Christabel," and the variety of stanza-structure in that poem gave him a hint of how he might present his own work. He wrote a few verses and then threw them into the fire. But friends pressed him to go on and he went on, " knowing no more than the man in the moon " how he was to end. A further hint was given to him that he might divide the poem into cantos and prefix each canto with a Spenserian motto. Recognising the " necessity of having some sort of pitch-pipe," Scott introduced the old harper as the teller of his tale and hence came *The Lay of the Last Minstrel*. It is a familiar story and it is rehearsed here not with a view to criticism of Scott's poetry, but as a reminder of the literary origins of the Author of *Waverley*.

As a poet, Scott was fully conscious both of his purpose and of his limitations. He had an intense desire to restore the currency of ballad-poetry and he was steeped in Scottish history and legend. He loved a drum and a soldier—especially in the Border country; he loved a ruined monastery or " the rudest remnant of a feudal tower " ; to his Gothic ear the *Stabat Mater* and the *Dies Irae* were more solemn and affecting than the classical poetry of Buchanan. " You have often given me materials for romance," he said once to his friend Morritt, " now I want a good robber's cave and an old church of the right sort." So Scott set out upon his poetic career with no illusions, but with something of the gaiety of a schoolboy. In his early days, at least, he liked to preserve his amateur status, and one of his reasons for refusing the Poet-Laureateship was that it could be more fittingly held by a professional poet like Southey.

> As for my own employment [he wrote in 1803], I have yet much before me, and as the beginning of letting out ink is like the letting out of water, I daresay I shall go on scribbling one nonsense or another to the end of the chapter. People may say this and that of the pleasure of fame or of profit as a motive of writing. I think the only pleasure is in the actual exertion and research. . . .

This is an approach as rare as it is refreshing—an approach very different from that search after " pure " or " poetic " poetry which is the subject of Housman's famous lecture; and yet there are times when Scott's verses seem to anticipate Housman himself:

> Proud Maisie is in the wood,
>   Walking so early;
> Sweet Robin sits on the bush,
>   Singing so rarely.
>
> " Tell me, thou bonny bird,
>   When shall I marry me ? "—
> " When six braw gentlemen
>   Kirkward shall carry ye."
>
> " Who makes the bridal bed,
>   Birdie, say truly ? "—
> " The grey-headed sexton
>   That delves the grave duly.
>
> " The glow-worm o'er grave and stone
>   Shall light thee steady;
> The owl from the steeple sing,
>   ' Welcome, proud lady.' "

In this and others of his shorter pieces Scott comes nearest to the heart of poetry. I will quote one more:

> The sun upon the lake is low,
> The wild birds hush their song,
> The hills have evening's deepest glow,
> Yet Leonard tarries long.
> Now all whom varied toil and care
> From home and love divide,
> In the calm sunset may repair
> Each to the loved one's side.

> The noble dame, on turret high,
> Who waits her gallant knight,
> Looks to the western beam to spy
> The flash of armour bright.
> The village maid, with hand on brow
> The level ray to shade,
> Upon the footpath watches now
> For Colin's darkening plaid.
>
> Now to their mates the wild swans row,
> By day they swam apart,
> And to the thicket wanders slow
> The hind beside the hart.
> The woodlark at his partner's side
> Twitters his closing song—
> All meet whom day and care divide,
> But Leonard tarries long!

The opening lines recall the very wording of "La Belle Dame sans Merci". Yet how different is the total effect. The picture presented by Scott's poem is clear and simple: in the quiet of evening lovers meet again—all but Leonard, who tarries long. But who was La Belle Dame sans Merci and what was the nameless terror that she inspired? "Poetry gives most pleasure," said Coleridge, "when only generally and not perfectly understood," and your thoroughgoing Romantic has no passion for perfect understanding.

When James Ballantyne asked Scott what he thought of his own genius in comparison with that of Burns, Scott was as indignant as was Housman when his scholarship was compared with that of Bentley: "There is no comparison whatever—we ought not to be named in the same day." "In fact," says Ballantyne, "he had often said to me that neither his own nor any modern popular style of composition was that from which he derived most pleasure. I asked him what it was. He answered—Johnson's; and that he had more pleasure in reading *London*, and *The Vanity of Human Wishes*, than any other poetical composition he could mention." For all his Gothic ear, Scott was at heart a good eighteenth-century man; it was, indeed, in the eighteenth century that Gothic ears were first cultivated.

With his fame as poet definitely established by the *Lay*, Scott, now a partner with James Ballantyne and no longer active at the Bar, turned his active mind to a multiplicity of literary projects. He undertook a new edition of Dryden and proposed a complete edition of British Poets, ancient and modern. "Much as I wish for a *corpus poetarum*," wrote his friend Ellis, "I should like still better another Minstrel Lay by the last and best Minstrel; and the general demand for the poem seems to prove that the public are of my opinion." Ellis was right, and *Marmion* was published in 1808. The poem was conceived, and written, with the author's characteristic gaiety and gusto. Each canto was preceded by an Introduction in which the poet allowed himself to be as topical, as topographical, and as autobiographical as he pleased. The Introduction to the third canto is addressed to William Erskine:

> For I was wayward, bold, and wild,
> A self-will'd imp, a grandame's child;
> But half a plague, and half a jest,
> Was still endured, beloved, caress'd.
>
> For me, thus nurtured, dost thou ask
> The classic poet's well-conn'd task?
> Nay, Erskine, nay—on the wild hill
> Let the wild heath-bell flourish still;
> Cherish the tulip, prune the vine,
> But freely let the woodbine twine,
> And leave, untrimm'd the eglantine:
> Nay, my friend, nay—since oft thy praise
> Hath given fresh vigour to my lays;
> Since oft thy judgment could refine
> My flatten'd thought, or cumbrous line;
> Still kind, as is thy wont, attend,
> And in the minstrel spare the friend.
> Though wild as cloud, as stream, as gale,
> Flow forth, flow unrestrain'd, my Tale!

Jeffrey, in the *Edinburgh Review*, warned Scott that, while his genius had brought chivalry into temporary favour, he must beware of the fickleness of fashion. But the tales flowed on, and when *The Lady of the Lake* was published in 1810, 20,000 copies were sold in a few months. There were more tales to come, but *The Lady of the Lake* was probably the high-water mark of Scott's reputation as a poet, and all the time his feet were on the ground.

> I have often thought [he wrote to Crabbe in 1813] it is the most fortunate thing for bards like you and me to have an established profession and professional

character, to render us independent of those worthy gentlemen, the retailers, or, as some have called them, the midwives of literature, whose shops are so littered with the abortions they bring into the world, that they are scarcely able to bestow the proper care upon young and flourishing babies like ours. . . . Did any of my sons show poetical talent, of which, to my great satisfaction, there are no appearances, the first thing I should do would be to inculcate upon him the duty of cultivating some honourable profession, and qualifying himself to play a more respectable part in society than the mere poet. . . . It is curious enough that you should have republished the " Village " for the purpose of sending your young men to college and I should have written the Lay of the Last Minstrel for the purpose of buying a new horse for the Volunteer Cavalry.

On the reference to " those worthy gentlemen, the retailers or midwives of literature," I make no comment. But here again Scott's eminently practical view of the writing of poetry is evident, and the time came when he recognised that the future lay with Lord Byron.

Meanwhile the Author of *Waverley* had been born. When the *Minstrelsy of the Scottish Border* had been published in 1802, one of the commentators had remarked that it contained " the elements of a hundred historical romances." He was speaking more truly than he knew. For about that time Scott had already " nourished the ambitious desire of composing a tale of chivalry . . . in the style of The Castle of Otranto, with plenty of Border characters and supernatural incident." Scott's own Introduction to *The Castle of Otranto*, like Gray's comment from

Cambridge that the book made them afraid to go to bed at night, shows how deep an influence Horace Walpole's story had upon his contemporaries—it was " the first modern attempt to found a tale of amusing fiction upon the basis of the ancient romances of chivalry." Fortunately, however, Border characters and Scottish history loomed larger in Scott's view than did supernatural incident. As early as 1805 he had contemplated an historical tale, but a tale of the recent past. In the Highlands he had personally met many veterans of the '45 who were " easily induced to fight their battles over again for the benefit of a willing listener." Seven chapters were written but were adversely criticised by a friend; they were put carefully into the drawer of an old writing-desk and lost. Admiration for Miss Edgeworth's Irish stories and Scott's own experience in editing and completing Joseph Strutt's romance, *Queenhoo Hall*, kept the idea fresh in his mind, but did not help him to find the lost chapters. Then, one day, he needed some fishing-tackle for a guest. The old writing-desk was ransacked and the manuscript was found. It is a familiar story—the story of one of the great and fortunate accidents which are so remarkable a feature of the history of the modern novel. There was Samuel Richardson, for instance, the respectable London printer who was invited by two worthy retailers of literature to compile a handbook of letter-writing for country bumpkins, but was eager to add something to illustrate the perils that beset a comely girl in domestic service and so produced *Pamela*, now firmly canonised in the text-books as the first modern novel; there was Henry Fielding, journalist, satirist and playwright, who seized upon *Pamela* as irresistible material for parody, wrote a few chapters in ludicrous imitation and then found his own true *métier* and laid the foundations on which the structure of English domestic fiction is built.

Scott's name is so indissolubly associated with the phrase " historical fiction," that it is important to remember that his first novel represented, in fact, a reaction from the romances of chivalry which had first captivated his youthful imagination. After editing *Queenhoo Hall* he realised that the manners of the Middle Ages did not possess the interest he had conceived, and he was " led to form the opinion that a romance, founded on a Highland story, and more modern events, would have a better chance of popularity than a tale of chivalry." Characteristically, there is little pride of artistry in his account of the completion of the story. He could not boast of having sketched any distinct plan of the work; nor could he claim that Waverley's movements up and down the country were managed with much skill. " It suited best, however," he says, " the road I wanted to travel." It was a road which was to become the scene of a long and triumphal procession.

Scott, in fact, was setting out upon a *via media*. Notwithstanding his Gothic ear and his love of the mystery and magic of the Middle Ages, he felt instinctively that if his projected romance was to "come home to Men's Businesse and Bosomes," it must concern itself with lives and manners that were not too remote and with places that he knew and loved with a natural intimacy. In his *Lives of the Novelists* and in his reviews of contemporary fiction, Scott traces the development of the novelist's art up to his own time. In his famous review of *Emma* he writes:

> The life of man rolls forth like a stream from the fountain, or it spreads out into tranquillity like a placid or stagnant lake. In the latter case, the individual grows old among the characters with whom he was born, and is contemporary,—shares precisely the sort of weal and woe to which his birth destined him,—moves in the same circle,—and, allowing for the change of seasons, is influenced by, and influences the same class of persons by which he was originally surrounded. The man of mark and of adventure, on the contrary, resembles, in the course of his life, the river whose mid-current and discharge into the ocean are widely removed from each other, as well as from the rocks and wild flowers which its fountains first reflected; violent changes of time, of place, and of circumstances, hurry him forward from one scene to another, and his adventures will usually be found only connected with each other because they have happened to the same individual. Such a history resembles an ingenious, fictitious narrative, exactly in the degree in which an old dramatic chronicle of the life and death of some distinguished character, where all the various agents appear and disappear as in the page of history, approaches a regular drama, in which every person introduced plays an appropriate part, and every point of the action tends to one common catastrophe.

So far as Scott's own novels are concerned, it is clear that he sought his material in the man of mark and of adventure who is hurried forward from one scene to another. Fertility of imagination and fluency of composition made such hurrying an easy and enjoyable process. When he came to contemplate the work of Miss Austen, Scott realised that " wild variety of incident " and " the splendid scenes of an imaginary world " were not part of her stock-in-trade and that she was much more easily vulnerable than the romantic author—" he who paints a scene of common occurrence, places his composition within that extensive range of criticism which general experience offers to every reader." And in *Emma* Scott recognised that notwithstanding the concentration upon " common incidents " and upon " such characters as occupy the ordinary walks of life," the author had achieved her purpose without the aid of " the excitation which depends upon a narrative of uncommon events." For his own part, Scott worked on a broad canvas. Some of his characters were ordinary, others were fantastic; sometimes he would go back a few decades and sometimes a few centuries; but, always, as Walter Raleigh noted, he sought verisimilitude rather than antiquarian accuracy.

The theme of *Waverley*, according to John Buchan, was " the impact upon the mind of an average educated Englishman of the alien world of the Scots Lowlands and the lingering mediaevalism of the Highlands." I beg leave to doubt whether the average English reader of 1814 was, in fact, precisely conscious of this impact. What he enjoyed was the pageantry of character to which the story introduced him. However that may be, what is more relevant is to examine what kind of an impression may be made on an average educated Englishman who reads *Waverley* for the first time at the present day. And here it is well to repeat what Scott himself so keenly realised. In 1814 the story was a little more than sixty years old; to-day it is two hundred years old. This is not to dispute the immortality of Scott; it is merely a reminder that elderly members of the reading public will in any generation seize with avidity upon a tale —provided it be a good tale and a well-written tale—which deals with a period which they can just remember. If next week there should appear a novel relating imaginatively, yet with reasonable verisimilitude, to the public events of the last decade of the nineteenth century (the Jubilees, Mr. Gladstone, Omdurman, the South African War), it would be judged on its merits as a novel. It might, or might not, make an immediate appeal to the novel-reader; but it would not be brushed aside with such a remark as, " Oh, I never read historical novels."

Time, " which antiquates antiquities, and hath an art to make dust of all things," has certainly not made dust of the Waverley Novels, but it has tended to put them in the category of books which no gentleman's library should be without. It also tends, or used to tend, to make them holiday-tasks for schoolboys. With slightly puckered brow, then, the ignorant reader, whether schoolboy or adult, turns to the first chapter of *Waverley* and what does he find? He finds that the title of the book " has not been chosen without the grave and solid deliberation which matters of importance demand from the prudent." It is then explained that the novel is neither a romance of chivalry nor a tale of modern manners, and that the author has endeavoured to throw the force of his narrative upon the characters and passions of the actors. " Good," says the novel-reader, " I am all for characters, and the more passionate, the better." Chapter II sketches the ancestry of Edward Waverley, and Chapter III his education, with some comments upon the decadent spoon-feeding which now passes as a substitute for solid instruction. (" The history of England is now reduced to a game at cards, the problems of mathematics to puzzles and riddles. . . ." It is curious how little educational criticism changes through the centuries.) Chapter IV tells of the family legends to which Waverley listened, and Chapter V of his being given a commission in the Dragoons. In Chapter VI, Waverley leaves his uncle's home to visit Cosmo Comyne Bradwardine of Bradwardine, and the story begins—but not without a substantial portion of topographical and architectural description. It may well be, indeed, that the beginner does not warm to his reading until, in Chapter X, the Baron orders the Château Margaux which he had shipped from Bordeaux in the year 1713. Certainly he will recognise that the Baron is one of those characters upon whom the force of the narrative depends:

"We cannot rival the luxuries of your English table, Captain Waverley, or give you the *epulae lautiores* of Waverley-Honour. I say *epulae* rather than *prandium*, because the latter phrase is popular: *epulae ad senatum, prandium vero ad populum attinet*, says Suetonius Tranquillus. But I trust ye will applaud my Boordeaux; *c'est des deux oreilles* as Captain Vinsauf used to say; *vinum primae notae*, the Principal of St. Andrews denominated it. And, once more, Captain Waverley, right glad am I that ye are here to drink the best my cellar can make forthcoming."

So, having applauded the Bordeaux, the reader is introduced to "the *leges conviviales*, or regulations of genial compotation," and later to the important distinction between *ebrii* and *ebrioli*.

Now I put the matter this way not with a view to cheap caricature, but to illustrate the preliminary obstacles to enjoyment that may arise in the first approach to the Waverley Novels. After all, the opening chapters of *Waverley* had been recognised as tedious by two of Scott's best friends, Erskine and James Ballantyne, when they read the first draft. Nevertheless, Ballantyne advised Scott to finish what he had begun. Never was there a more willing craftsman in the workshop of literature. "I love," he wrote in later years, "to have the press thumping, clattering and banging in my rear," and the second and third volumes of *Waverley* were written in three weeks. "I had a great deal of fun," Scott wrote to Morritt, "in the accomplishment of this task."

Here one may pause a moment for a gasp of admiring astonishment. *Waverley* was written at a time when Scott was still spending five hours a day in court. Judged by any normal standard of literary composition, he achieved the impossible. Lockhart's famous story of the hand which distracted the hour of his friends' hilarity has a slightly tragic ring:

> It fascinates my eye—it never stops—page after page is finished and thrown on that heap of MS., and still it goes on unwearied—and so it will be till candles are brought in and God knows how long after that. It is the same every night—I can't stand a sight of it. . . .

But it was Scott's way of having fun; and when the book was finished he was adamant in insisting that it should be published anonymously. In part, his motive was prudential, for anonymity might be an insurance against failure; but at the bottom of it was the desire for more fun, and later he had the additional fun of being his own reviewer.

I have ventured to entitle this lecture, " The Making of a Novelist," but when one contemplates the ease and rapidity and gaiety with which the later part of *Waverley* was written, one wonders whether a better title would not have been " A Novelist Ready-made." For though Scott had not written a novel before, he knew a lot about the habits of novel-readers. He knew that they commonly skipped the preface and that they read the last chapter first. So he cunningly inserted his preface at the end of the book, and in it he explained what he had primarily aimed to achieve—a picture both of the Highlands and of the Lowlands as they had been two generations back and a series of honest portraits of their inhabitants illustrating, without caricature or exaggeration, their habits, manners and feelings.

It is a common criticism of Scott that his dialogue is markedly superior to his description, and passages selected from *Waverley* almost at random may well illustrate the comparison. Take, for instance, Waverley's meeting with Flora:

> Eddying round this reservoir, the brook found its way as if over a broken part of the ledge, and formed a second fall, which seemed to seek the very abyss; then, wheeling out beneath from among the smooth dark rocks, which it had polished for ages, it wandered murmuring down the glen, forming the stream up which Waverley had just ascended. The borders of this romantic reservoir corresponded in beauty; but it was beauty of a stern and commanding cast, as if in the act of expanding into grandeur. Mossy banks of turf were broken and interrupted by huge fragments of rock, and decorated with trees and shrubs, some of which had been planted under the direction of Flora, but so cautiously, that they added to the grace, without diminishing the romantic wildness of the scene.

In passages of this kind the effortless fluency of Scott's narrative becomes a positive disadvantage. No doubt he had an actual scene in mind (he tells us so in a note), and the description is in the manner of a romantic guide-book to the Highlands with Flora introduced in the guise of Capability Brown. But now for Flora herself:

Here like one of those lovely forms which decorate the landscapes of Poussin, Waverley found Flora gazing on the waterfall. Two paces farther back stood Cathleen, holding a small Scottish harp, the use of which had been taught to Flora by Rory Dall, one of the last harpers of the Western Highlands. The sun, now stooping in the west, gave a rich and varied tinge to all the objects which surrounded Waverley, and seemed to add more than human brilliancy to the full expressive darkness of Flora's eye, exalted the richness and purity of her complexion, and enhanced the dignity and grace of her beautiful form. Edward thought he had never, even in his wildest dreams, imagined a figure of such exquisite and interesting loveliness. The wild beauty of the retreat, bursting upon him as if by magic, augmented the mingled feeling of delight and awe with which he approached her, like a fair enchantress of Boiardo or Ariosto, by whose nod the scenery around seemed to have been created, an Eden in the wilderness.

Here is all the bookishness of the romantic cult. Who cares about the identity of Flora's music-teacher? What young lover, as he approaches his beloved, stops to think about waterfalls and Ariosto?

On the other hand, turn to Charles Edward's first words of greeting to Waverley:

" I desire to gain no adherents save from affection and conviction; and if Mr Waverley inclines to prosecute his journey to the south, or to join the forces of the Elector, he shall have my passport and free permission to do so; and I can only regret, that my present power will not extend to protect him against the probable consequences of such a measure. But . . . if Mr. Waverley should, like his ancestor, Sir Nigel, determine to embrace a cause which has little to recommend it but its justice, and follow a prince who throws himself upon the affections of his people to recover the throne of his ancestors, or perish in the attempt, I can only say, that among these nobles and gentlemen he will find worthy associates in a gallant enterprise, and will follow a master who may be unfortunate, but, I trust, will never be ungrateful."

Here is the measured dignity and clarity of Augustan prose, the prose of Dr. Johnson's prefaces. And Edward Waverley answered simply by falling on to his knees. It was not for him to bandy civilities with his sovereign.

The *Edinburgh Review* had been critical of Scott's romantic poems, but it had no doubts about *Waverley*. In the grand manner of those days it devoted 35 pages to the book, most of them filled with extracts, but opening with intelligent praise:

It is wonderful what genius and adherence to nature will do, in spite of all disadvantages. Here is a thing obviously very hastily, and, in many places, very unskilfully written . . . relating to a period too recent to be romantic, and too far gone by to be familiar . . . and yet, by the mere force and truth and vivacity of its colouring, already casting the whole tribe of ordinary novels into the shade . . . The secret of this success, we take it, is merely that the author is a person of genius.

Nor had Jeffrey any doubt about the authorship: " If it be indeed the work of an author hitherto unknown," he wrote, " Mr. Scott would do well to look to his laurels, and to rouse himself for a sturdier competition than any he has yet had to encounter." The *Quarterly*, on the other hand, opened patronisingly:

> We have had so many occasions to invite our readers' attention to that species of composition called Novels and have so often stated our general views of the principles of this very agreeable branch of literature, that we shall venture on the consideration of our present subject with but a few observations, and those applicable to a class of novels, of which it is a favourable specimen.

Since historians of criticism, in deploring the poor quality of contemporary reviewing, sometimes refer nostalgically to the great days of the *Edinburgh* and the *Quarterly*, it is well to recall occasionally the windy jargon of which these periodicals were capable. The *Quarterly*'s final paragraph on *Waverley* is as wrong-headed as it is pompous:

> We confess that we have, speaking generally, a great objection to what may be called historical romance, in which real and fictitious personages, and actual and fabulous events are mixed together to the utter confusion of the reader . . . and we cannot but wish that the ingenious and intelligent author of Waverley had rather employed himself in recording *historically* the character and transactions of his countrymen *Sixty Years since*, than in writing a work, which, though it may be, in its facts, almost true, and in its delineations perfectly accurate, will yet, in sixty years *hence*, be regarded, or rather, probably, *disregarded*, as a *mere* romance, and the gratuitous invention of a facetious fancy.

A reviewer who indulges in prophecy always invites disaster, but it is difficult to imagine anything more inept than the *Quarterly*'s verdict upon

Waverley. Who cares about the accurate record of historical transactions? *Waverley* lives by the virtue of the romantic colour of its characterisation.

It was characteristic of Scott that he should immediately embark upon a second novel. *The Lord of the Isles* had just been published, and although it was in fact far from being a failure, James Ballantyne could not conceal his disappointment at its reception. But Scott refused to be depressed. "Since one line has failed," he said, "we must just stick to something else." So he stuck to his desk for six weeks and produced *Guy Mannering*. There can be but one comment, and that Dominie Sampson's — Prodigious! Again, it was characteristic of the freshness and fertility of Scott's invention that this second novel should be wholly different from his first. He plunged straight into his tale and introduced the reader, without historical preliminaries, to what Lockhart calls "a new group of immortal realities"—among them Meg Merrilies, that figure of wild and poetic grandeur who, like many other figures from among the common people, exhibits Scott's powers at their highest:

"Ride your ways, ride your ways, Laird of Ellangowan. . . . This day have ye quenched seven smoking hearths—see if the fire in your ain parlour burn the blyther for that. Ye have riven the thack off seven cottar houses—look if your ain roof-tree stand the faster . . ."

The Novelist was made.

II
THE FATE OF A NOVELIST

In the catalogue of a second-hand bookseller received some time last year I find the following item:

Scott (Sir Walter) Waverley Novels, complete run from the start to 1826 (does not include Chronicles of Canongate, Anne of Geierstein, Tales Landlord, 4th series, which came later). All First Editions except—Waverley, Rob Roy, The Monastery, in all 62 vols, *half calf, very few half-titles,* but quite a number of early points or cancels in the original state; binding somewhat rubbed, clean within, not a set for the fastidious collector but very suitable for a student of early editions, University, Public Library or some similar home of literary research, 1814 etc. £12, 12s.

And a kindred item follows:

Scott (Sir Walter) Life of, by Lockhart, portraits, 7 vols, 8vo, First Edition, 1837. 35s.

To the description of this second item the bookseller adds a comment of his own:

The second greatest biography, and one of the most lovable and readable books in our language, and here is the first edition for 35s. Surely this is a chance to take advantage of the whims of fashion.

This little note is clearly inspired by something more than motives of salesmanship. The bookseller probably had in mind that in the earlier pages of his catalogue a copy of the greatest of English biographies—also written by a Scotsman—was offered for sale at a price of £80; he was probably reflecting, also, that the twelve guineas which he was prepared to take for the 62 volumes of the Waverley Novels would only go a little way towards the cost of a really good copy of the first edition, say, of *Barchester Towers* or of *Tess of the D'Urbervilles*.

Clearly something has happened. It is true that the first edition of *Waverley* itself is a collector's piece, but for the rest of the novels there is little enthusiasm or extravagance in the sale-room. Of course, this is not the whole story. Collectors, with their " whims of fashion " are not the arbiters of literary value. The records of public libraries make it clear that the Waverley Novels are still being widely read and publishers are still engaged in producing them in the form of cheap reprints. But the fact remains that during the last twenty years neither amongst readers nor amongst collectors has there been any revival of enthusiasm for Scott such as there has been, for instance, for Anthony Trollope. And if it should be argued that the prejudices and absurdities of the book-collector are of no account, it should be remembered that, in the main, the collector follows public taste—he does not determine it. Forty years ago no collector worried about Trollope. For twenty years after the posthumous publication of his *Autobiography* in 1883 he was an author whom there were none to praise and very few to love. Then, in the first decade of the present century, critics began the process of reinstatement, and in the nineteen-twenties the revival was in full swing. Cheap reprints appeared, some of them of books that had not been in print for sixty or seventy years; and there is nothing like a cheap reprint to whet the collector's appetite for a first edition. That is the point at which " rarity value " begins to displace literary criteria. First editions of Trollope's famous books fetch high prices; but his two forgotten first novels are of such rarity that they command any price that competing collectors, in their mad pride of bibliophily, may be prepared to give.

This is not an essay upon the vagaries of connoisseurship; but comparative values in the sale-room are, in fact, as good a starting-point as any other for a consideration of Scott's place in the estimation of recent generations of the reading public as compared with that of Trollope.

Now Scott and Trollope had at least one characteristic in common: each wrote honestly about himself and about his manner of writing. Trollope was at pains to emphasise that a man who devoted himself to literature with industry and perseverance could succeed, and was entitled to succeed, in gaining a livelihood like any other man in any other profession. Scott used almost the same words: " Cant set apart," he wrote, " it is the same thing with literary emoluments. No man of sense, in any rank of life, is, or ought to be, above accepting a just recompense for his time, and a reasonable share of the capital which owes its very existence to his exertions."

Trollope shocked the readers of his *Autobiography* by describing how he wrote with his watch in front of him and set himself to write 250 words every quarter of an hour; Scott in his *Journal* similarly describes, without sentimentality and without self-pity, how he disciplined himself to write his daily quota of pages in order to pay off his creditors.

But while Scott came to the writing of prose fiction somewhat tentatively through the media of Border ballads and of his own poems, Trollope deliberately cherished a determination to become a writer of novels at a comparatively early stage in his career. When he entered the Civil Service, he had read Shakespeare and Byron and Scott; he thought *Pride and Prejudice* was the best novel in the language, but eventually it had to yield to *Ivanhoe* and *Esmond*. He had been made a Post Office Surveyor in Ireland and had begun his work there at the age of twenty-nine. Stationed at a village in County Leitrim, he was led to the writing of his first book by just such a scene as, *mutatis mutandis*, would have attracted and stimulated Scott:

> As we were taking a walk in that most uninteresting country, we turned up through a deserted gateway, along a weedy, grass-grown avenue, till we came to the modern ruins of a country house. It was one of the most melancholy spots I ever visited. . . . While I was still among the ruined walls and decayed beams I fabricated the plot of *The Macdermotts of Ballycloran*.

Trollope thought, and continued to think, that

the plot was a good one, but he expected the book to fail. His expectations were fulfilled. His second novel, *The Kellys and the O'Kellys*, suffered a similar fate—in Ireland it was not only not read, but never heard of. But it did get one review in *The Times*:

> Of *The Kellys and the O'Kellys* we may say what the master said to the footman, when the man complained of the constant supply of legs of mutton on the kitchen table. "Well, John, legs of mutton are good substantial food"; and we may say also what John replied: "Substantial, sir—yes, they are substantial, but a little coarse."

140 copies of the book were sold.

All this is very different from the tumultuous reception of *Waverley* and *Guy Mannering*. But Scott's first two novels were, in one sense, a climax of achievement; Trollope's were works of apprenticeship. It was a walk round the cathedral at Salisbury on a midsummer evening that was to bring him inspiration and immortality—not that he flattered himself about either of these attainments: he was prepared to believe that *Barchester Towers* might be read for a quarter of a century; as for inspiration, he preferred to accept the maxim that the surest aid to the writing of a book was a piece of cobbler's wax on the writer's chair. Nor was he ashamed to confess that, while he was not insensitive to the charms of literary reputation, his first object in writing was to make an income on which he and his family could live in comfort. He enjoyed the actual work of writing and found that he could do it quite comfortably in railway carriages. As soon as one novel was finished, he was fully prepared to begin another.

Thus, in Trollope's circumstances and temperament there is, in spite of obvious contrasts, a good deal that is reminiscent of Scott: there is the same realistic approach to the profession of authorship; the same fertility of production; the same love of good company; the same devotion to manly sports and exercises. On the other hand, although Trollope embarked upon several pieces of historical writing and upon one historical novel, he had no wistful day-dreams of feudal glory. For Scott, Abbotsford was the embodiment of his ambition to establish himself as a latter-day baron of the Border country; Trollope had no desire for a stately mansion in Barsetshire—£4500 a year and the Garrick Club were good enough for him. It is the difference, perhaps, between the romantic visions of the dawn, and the comfortable prosperity of the middle, of the nineteenth century.

It has, in recent years, become a commonplace of criticism to assign to Trollope a supreme place in what is called the " literature of escape," an unfortunate phrase used too glibly to be of any critical value. Escape from what? Escape into what? If it means simply escape from the routine and anxieties of everyday life into a world of the imagination, is not all literature, all drama, all music, all art, in short, a means of such escape? Or does the literature of escape mean the reading of such books as will provide entertainment and amusement without any kind of intellectual stimulus, books which will enable us to see and feel, but will not trouble us to think? Is it just the difference between *The Merry Wives of Windsor* and *Hamlet*? Or must the gulf be wider, the gulf, say, between P. G. Wodehouse and H. G. Wells? No doubt the phrase has been popularised by the times in which we have lived. Anyone who can remember reading, say, *Pride and Prejudice*, in a leaky dug-out in France in 1917, has a fair notion of its significance in particular circumstances. In short, the phrase " escapist literature " may be regarded as one of the many unfortunate by-products of our latest age of strife and bewilderment.

But, if the phrase is a product of our own age, there is nothing new in the critical attitude which has provoked it. At the beginning of the nineteenth century, the novel as a literary *genre* was still suspect and was frowned upon both by Puritans and by highbrows. Zachary Macaulay forbade novel-reading in the day-time—" drinking drams in the morning " he called it; Crabb Robinson wrote in his diary: " *Guy Mannering* is a work of higher interest than the author's *Waverley*, but is not, like that, connected with history, and therefore will be less read by the grave class of readers who want an apology for opening a novel "; Coleridge in a scornful footnote likened the reading of novels and tales of chivalry to such other amusements as " swaying on a chair or gate; spitting over a bridge; smoking; snuff taking; *tête-à-tête* quarrels after dinner between husband and wife." But what is more pertinent is Coleridge's view of the Waverley Novels. Coleridge said many things in praise of Scott and in particular of his universality. In the portrayal by the Author of Waverley of Jacobites and Calvinists he saw something more than a representation of a particular struggle in a particular century. It was a picture, he said, of " the contest between the two great moving principles of social humanity: religious adherence to the past and the passion for truth as the offspring of reason." But at the same time he attributed the popularity of the novels to the fact that they provided amusement " without requiring any effort of thought and without exciting any deep emotion. . . ." The universal excitement aroused by the extraordinary events of the time, he says, demanded relaxation.

Fortes ante Agamemnona. Earlier generations endured wars and tumults and took refuge in " escapist " literature, but, happily, they did not have a word for it.

If evidence were required of the abiding interest in Scott and his work throughout the nineteenth century, it would of course be found quite simply by turning to any well-established critic of the period. Carlyle in his famous review of Lockhart's *Life*, remarked: " With respect to the literary character of these Waverley Novels, so extraordinary in their commercial character, there remains, after so much reviewing, good and bad, little that it were profitable at present to say." And then Carlyle goes on to say it at considerable length. For him, too, the Waverley Novels were for the reader lying on a sofa; they were not a part of that Literature which is " the Thought of Thinking Souls "—a dictum with which the Author of Waverley would heartily, and thankfully, have agreed.

A greater critic than Carlyle, William Hazlitt, dismissed Scott's poetry as superficial and fulminated, with vast rhetorical exaggeration, against his politics; but about the Waverley Novels he has no doubts:

> What a host of associations! What a thing is human life! What a power is that of genius! . . . It is no wonder that the public repay with lengthened applause and gratitude the pleasure they receive. He writes as fast as they can read, and he does not write himself down. He is always in the public eye and we do not tire of him. . . .

This was in 1824, and for twenty years or more there was little or no sign of the public growing tired. In 1848 Cadell referred with satisfaction to the ceaseless demand for the novels—" every hour, every minute of the day some one of them is called for," and in the following year the Reverend H. Mackenzie, Vicar of St. Martin's-in-the-Fields, stated in evidence before the Select Committee on Public Libraries that he had found some of the younger subscribers to the library in his parish difficult to get to church on Sunday, because they were reading Walter Scott's novels.

But after another twenty years the taste of the novel-reader had been deflected into different channels. A *Quarterly* reviewer of 1863 faced with two dozen " sensation novels " (including *Lady Audley's Secret* and Wilkie Collins's *No Name*) sadly remarks : " We have known young persons, familiar with the latest products of the circulating library, who not only had never read Scott, but who had no idea that he was worth reading," and five years later we read in the same journal : " Scott seems to be in danger of passing—we cannot conceive why—out of the knowledge of the rising generation "—a comment which seems to bring us right down to the present day.

In 1827 Christopher North had scornfully dismissed the notion that Scott would not be read in a hundred years' time, since " the passions that played their parts in his grand fictions were primary and permanent." In 1927 Mr. E. M. Forster delivered a course of lectures at Cambridge which he entitled " Aspects of the Novel," and in his second lecture he declared :

> Scott is a novelist over whom we shall violently divide. For my own part I do not care for him. . . . He is seen to have a trivial mind and a heavy style. He cannot construct. He has neither artistic detachment nor passion, and how can a writer who is devoid of both, create characters who will move us deeply ? . . . If he had passion, he would be a great writer— no amount of clumsiness or artificiality would matter then. But he only has a temperate heart and gentlemanly feelings, and an intelligent affection for the country-side : and this is not basis enough for great novels.

It is to be noted that Mr. Forster does not suggest that Scott's reputation has vanished. On the contrary, he offers two reasons for its continuance: first, many people love his books because they heard them read aloud in their youth (Mr. Forster himself loves *The Swiss Family Robinson* for this reason), and secondly, Scott " could tell a story. He had the primitive power of keeping the reader in suspense and playing on his curiosity."

On the argument of sentimental reminiscence we need not linger. The second argument, that Scott could tell a story, might seem to the unsophisticated reader to be something in his favour. But here it has to be remembered that Mr. Forster has a quarrel—no, quarrel is too strong a word, he has a drooping regret that story-telling is an essential part of the novelist's task. To make his position clear, I must quote the page with which his lecture opens:

We shall all agree that the fundamental aspect of the novel is its story-telling aspect, but we shall voice our assent in different tones. . . . Let us listen to three voices. If you ask one type of man, " What does a novel do ? " he will reply placidly: " Well,—I don't know . . . I suppose it kind of tells a story, so to speak." He is quite good tempered and vague, and probably driving a motor-bus at the same time and paying no more attention to literature than it merits. Another man, whom I visualize as on a golf-course, will be aggressive and brisk. He will reply: " What does a novel do ? Why, tell a story of course, and I've no use for it if it didn't. I like a story. Very bad taste on my part, no doubt, but I like a story. You can take your art, you can take your literature, you can take your music, but give me a good story. And I like a story to be a story, mind, and my wife's the same." And a third man he says in a sort of drooping regretful voice, " Yes—oh dear yes—the novel tells a story." I respect and admire the first speaker. I detest and fear the second. And the third is myself. Yes—oh dear yes—the novel tells a story.

Clearly a critic who starts from these premises is not likely to have much more sympathy with Scott than he has with the golf-course, and when Mr. Forster paraphrases *The Antiquary* in a few pages, he can make it seem very small beer. Lovel, he says, meets the Antiquary and visits him at his house. Near it they meet a new character, Edie Ochiltree. " Scott is good," he goes on, " at introducing fresh characters. He slides them in very naturally, and with a promising air. Edie Ochiltree promises a good deal. . . ." Then some legitimate fun is poked at the somewhat stilted description of Sir Arthur Wardour and his daughter being cut off by the tide. After a scornful reference to Lovel's dream in the haunted room, Mr. Forster records the treasure-hunts organised by Dousterswivel and the sudden appearance of the Glenallans. Finally, he summarises the complications of the concluding chapters of the book. " There are indeed," he says, " plenty of reasons for the dénouement, but Scott is not interested in reasons; he dumps them down without bothering to elucidate them; to make one thing happen after another is his only serious aim."

Now this is entertaining, but it is not fair, criticism. Indeed, it is not meant to be. Mr.

Forster was deliberately provocative and hoped to rouse the opposition of at least part of his audience.

Of course it is true that Scott set out to tell a story; it is also true that he frequently grew weary of its ramifications and was uncertain how to finish it. In *The Antiquary* the sudden appearance of the Glenallan family burying their Countess is clumsy and abrupt and points to a definite failure in construction. Scott had neither the time nor the inclination to tie together all the loose ends of his narrative. In *The Antiquary*, in particular, he claims that he was not primarily concerned with adventure and romance: " If a man will paint from nature," he said, " he will be likely to amuse those who are daily looking at it." What he enjoyed in *The Antiquary* was the painting of such portraits as those of Edie Ochiltree, Dousterswivel, the Mucklebackits and Oldbuck himself. Take away those portraits and the story is not worth reading. Who, for instance, wants to spend time over Lovel's courtship of Miss Wardour ?

" I am much embarrassed, Mr. Lovel," replied the young lady, " by your—I would not willingly use a strong word—your romantic and hopeless pertinacity— It is for yourself I plead, that you would consider the calls which your country has upon your talents, that you will not waste, in an idle and fanciful indulgence of an ill-placed predilection, time, which, well redeemed by active exertion, should lay the foundation of future distinction—let me entreat you that you would form a manly resolution "—

" It is enough, Miss Wardour . . ."

It is indeed.

On the other hand, consider Edie Ochiltree's first appearance. Oldbuck has been describing to Lovel the discovery of a sculptured stone bearing the letters A.D.L.L. which might stand, " without much violence," for *Agricola Dicavit Libens Lubens*.

" Yes, my dear friend, from this stance it is probable, —nay it is nearly certain, that Julius Agricola beheld what our Beaumont has so admirably described !—From this very Praetorium "—

And then the deflation :

" Praetorian here, Praetorian there, I mind the bigging o't."

and A.D.L.L. is shown to stand for " Aiken Drum's Lang Ladle."

Mr. Forster's complaint of the idiotic marriage with which the story ends is of course a complaint not against *The Antiquary* but against every romantic novel that was ever written and, in general, his view of Scott is far from being representative of modern criticism as a whole.

Virginia Woolf (so lucid as a critic, so puzzling as a novelist) approaches *The Antiquary* in a spirit of affectionate gaiety. She recognises at once the faults of style and language—" the old metaphors out of the property-box " that " come flapping their dusty wings across the sky " ; the stilted phraseology which smothers the reality of passionate love-making ; the careless construction as if Scott's parts " come together without his willing it." But at the same time she remains entranced not by the story, but by the old friends she meets in the story:

> However often one may have read *The Antiquary*, Jonathan Oldbuck is slightly different every time. We notice different things; our observation of face and voice differs; and thus Scott's characters, like Shakespeare's and Jane Austen's, have the seed of life in them.

But there is a qualification:

> Scott's characters . . . suffer from a serious disability; it is only when they speak that they are alive; they never think; as for prying into their minds himself or drawing inferences from their behaviour, Scott never attempted it. . . .

Here, of course, we come to the great gulf between Scott and those modern novelists who spend so much time prying into their characters' minds that they frequently forget that they may be expected to tell a story. The story—oh dear yes—the story. But Virginia Woolf solves the problem by an easy dualism:

> Either Scott the novelist is swallowed whole and becomes part of the body and brain, or he is rejected entirely. There is no middle party . . .

This, surely, is over-simplification. Certainly there is in this year of grace a substantial body of readers which neglects Scott—it appears to have been in existence since the 1860's. In the United States, I am told, such neglect is general except in the Southern States, where any suggestion of a neo-feudal society is popular. But of those who still read and enjoy the Waverley Novels, can it be said that they all swallow them whole in an ecstasy of gluttonous enthusiasm? In 1932, the year in which the centenary of Scott's death was celebrated, the enthusiasts very naturally were busy: there was the series of essays from *The Times Literary Supplement* by Thomas Seccombe and others; the new *Life* by John Buchan; the collection of retrospective studies edited by Sir Herbert Grierson, followed later by his standard edition of the *Letters* and by his own biography, embodying valuable corrections of, and additions to, Lockhart's narrative. These and many other tributes were the work of readers and admirers of Scott. But they were not wholly uncritical and, *pace* Virginia Woolf, I incline to the view that there is a middle course taken by a large number of cultivated readers at the present time. Such readers are frankly eclectic. Many of them were advised to read *Ivanhoe* or *Quentin Durward* in their youth—with discouraging results. Later they have come to choose for themselves and they read *Guy Mannering* or *The Antiquary* or *Redgauntlet* for the sake of the great gallery of characters to be met in their pages. Such readers may not be familiar with more than half a dozen novels in all, but they are not entirely neglectful. That, I conjecture, may be taken as Scott's fate as a novelist—south of the Border. Scott himself would not have been dismayed. "Horace himself," he wrote, "expected not to survive in all his works. *Non omnis moriar.*"

At this point I return to Trollope. For in the Trollope revival eclecticism has virtually disappeared. Trollope's frankness about his royalties and his regular output placed him under a cloud for many years and even his obituarists were lukewarm: " He could not manage very deep passion," wrote *The Times*, " and had the sense rarely to attempt it. . . . No deep riddles, no unconquerable troubles diversified Mr. Trollope's stories. . . . It would be rash to prophesy that his work will long be read. . . ." But when the tide turned, it was a spring tide. People clamoured, and are clamouring, not only for the Barchester novels, or for the political series, but for everything that Trollope ever wrote. Passionate appeals have been made, especially from the United States (where a quarterly journal, *The Trollopian*, is now published), for a definitive edition of his collected works that should be worthy of his genius.

When Trollope conceived the story of *The Warden* in the course of his walk round the cathedral at Salisbury, he had no intimate, or even casual acquaintance with ecclesiastical dignitaries. He had certain views of his own about the use and abuse of ecclesiastical endowments, but he had made no serious study of Church history, he had never even spoken to an archdeacon. Consequently the opening chapter of *Barchester Towers* has been severely criticised by those who are more familiar with the procedure in episcopal appointments than Trollope ever pretended to be. But technical inaccuracy has not marred the common reader's enjoyment of the troubles of Archdeacon Grantly and the machinations of Mrs. Proudie. Trollope's characters were his own creation, and when they were re-discovered they became more popular than at their first appearance. Why? First, because they had acquired a mellow flavour of the past without being entirely antiquated. To readers of Trollope in the nineteen-twenties Barchester was but sixty years since, and although certain changes had come over life in a cathedral city, the life was still going on. Some readers might well recall an uncle who was not wholly unlike Archdeacon Grantly; they might even more vividly remember a great-aunt who possessed, in a milder degree, some of the qualities of Mrs. Proudie. On the other hand, those emancipated readers who tended to look upon deans and archdeacons as museum pieces, keenly relished the characters in the Barchester novels as picturesque survivals of the ages of Victorian faith.

Thus to a great company of English readers Trollope's world was easy of access. Scott's world, on the other hand, was more remote; it lay for the most part across the Border and across the centuries. And there are other factors. Imagine, for instance, a tyro who has been advised, as well he may be, to embark upon the reading of *The Heart of Midlothian*. He secures a modern edition without difficulty and opens the book. He finds, first, an Introduction which describes the incident on which the story is founded; there follows a Postscript to this narrative; after that comes a Prolegomenon addressed to the Courteous Reader by Jedediah

Cleishbotham, and to this is added a footnote of several pages in small type in which the ghost of the author's grandmother arises to speak the epilogue. Now it is perfectly true that the Discourteous Reader may skip all this and begin at Chapter I. Even if he does so, he will find that that chapter is also introductory, recording how a mail-coach accident brought together two lawyers and an unfortunate litigant who discover between them that the Tolbooth of Edinburgh might supply material "far beyond what the boldest novelist ever attempted to produce from the coinage of his brain." So, with a hopeful feeling that he has witnessed the final prologue, our novice looks forward to the opening of the drama. He turns to Chapter II which gives an account of the events of 7th September 1736, when preparations were made for the execution of two smugglers and one escaped. Chapter III, with its description of Captain John Porteous and the Edinburgh City Guard, recalls to him a name that he once encountered in a history text-book, and in Chapter IV some of the characters begin to emerge from the turmoil of the Porteous Riots.

Now, if a novel is to have an historical background, it may well be argued that Scott's vivid description of the Porteous Riots forms a fine setting for the opening of his romance. But, as Professor Pottle has remarked, " Scott, having presented a romance, seems almost to feel under obligation to deflate it by parallel columns of history," and the novel reader of to-day may well be forgiven if he pleads for a simpler and more direct approach. So let us suppose that instead of *The Heart of Midlothian*, he takes up a copy of *The Last Chronicle of Barset*. Chapter I is entitled, very simply, " How did he get it ? " and begins :

" I can never bring myself to believe it, John," said Mary Walker, the pretty daughter of Mr. George Walker, attorney of Silverbridge. Walker and Winthrop was the name of the firm, and they were respectable people, who did all the solicitors' business that had to be done in that part of Barsetshire on behalf of the Crown, were employed on the local business of the Duke of Omnium who is great in those parts, and altogether held their heads up high, as provincial lawyers often do. They—the Walkers—lived in a great brick house in the middle of the town, gave dinners, to which the county gentlemen not unfrequently condescended to come, and in a mild way led the fashion in Silverbridge. " I can never bring myself to believe it, John," said Miss Walker.

" You'll have to bring yourself to believe it," said John, without taking his eyes from his book.

" A clergyman—and such a clergyman, too."

" I don't see that that has anything to do with it." And as he now spoke, John did take his eyes off his book. " Why should not a clergyman turn thief as well as anybody else ? You girls always seem to forget that clergymen are only men after all."

" Their conduct is likely to be better than that of other men, I think."

" I deny it utterly," said John Walker. " I'll undertake to say that at this moment there are more clergymen in debt in Barsetshire than there are either lawyers or doctors. This man has always been in debt. Since he has been in the county I don't think he has ever been able to show his face in the High Street of Silverbridge."

"John, that is saying more than you have a right to say," said Mrs. Walker.

Now this is not distinguished writing. Taken by itself, the page that I have quoted might be the beginning of a novelette. In fact, it is the beginning of the story of the Reverend Mr. Crawley, the only man who ever silenced Mrs. Proudie. "In the invention of Crawley," wrote Q, "I protest that I am astonished almost as though he [Trollope] had suddenly shown himself capable of inventing a King Lear."

This is not to set up *The Last Chronicle of Barset* as a finer novel than *The Heart of Midlothian*. They are not comparable. But if Scott had opened his tale with a conversation in Mr. Saddletree's shop instead of deferring it to the middle of his fourth chapter, *The Heart of Midlothian* might have more readers to-day.

Trollope himself had in his early days tried his hand at an historical novel. He received £20 on account of the first 350 copies of *La Vendée*, but he heard no more of it. When, a few years later, he was waiting in a publisher's office with the manuscript of *The Three Clerks* under his arm, the foreman of the house ventured a little advice: "I hope it's not historical, Mr. Trollope? Whatever you do, don't be historical; your historical novel is not worth a damn." That was in 1857. Times had changed since a new work by the Author of Waverley had been an outstanding event in a publishing season. Trollope, of course, wrote with contemporary history in mind, especially in his political novels, but Barchester was his own creation, independent of any particular locality or of any particular group of ecclesiastical dignitaries and landed gentry. Trollope grew progressively fonder of his characters and the affection is transmitted to his readers. It is true that Trollope, like Scott and all novelists on the grand scale, has his *longueurs*; the opening chapter of *Orley Farm*, for instance, is intolerably tedious and confusing. But to open a Barchester novel is to feel like rejoining a family party. The narrative requires no historical or topographical annotation, though in later days it has invited something of the kind. More than one Trollopian has constructed a map of Barsetshire.

Lastly, Trollope is profoundly English. " These books," said Hawthorne, " are just as English as a beef-steak. . . . It needs an English residence to make them thoroughly comprehensible "—and similarly the Englishman reading Scott must frequently feel that even when he is enjoying the narrative, he cannot savour it in the true spirit of a connoisseur, the spirit, for instance, of Andrew Lang's loyal address in his collection of *Letters to Dead Authors*. There Scott is apostrophised in the heart of his own country and among his own grey, round-shouldered hills, where each legend of burn and loch combined to inform his spirit.

This is not to suggest either that Scott survives only in the Border country or that Trollope can be appreciated only by natives of Barsetshire;

but it does tempt one to speculate for a moment upon what might have happened if chance had led Scott to spend a year or two of his life in an English country town. Scott's criticism of the English character is always genial and frequently affectionate. The enjoyment with which, in his early days, he reviewed that remarkable work *The Miseries of Human Life*, by the Reverend James Beresford, is evident. The typically English humour of the book made an immediate appeal to him:

> The Englishman [he writes] feels the satisfaction of grumbling over his misfortunes to be, on many occasions, so much greater than the pain of enduring them, that he will beg, borrow, or steal, or even manufacture calamities, sooner than suffer under any unusual scarcity of discontent. He knows, indeed, that miseries are necessary to his happiness, and though perhaps not quite so pleasant at the moment as his other indispensable enjoyments, roast beef and beer, would, if taken away, leave just as great a craving in his appetites as would be occasioned by the privation of these national dainties.

But if he laughed at "the English Malady," Scott had a special regard for the Anglican Church and the Anglican clergy. English parish churches seemed to him to be "the most cleanly, decent and reverential places of worship . . . to be found in the Christian world"; and Jeanie Deans could not help noting, with some reluctance, the superiority of "the irregular, yet extensive and commodious pile" that constituted an English rectory to the manses as she knew them in her own country.

Suppose, then, that Scott, with his quick perception and his fluent pen, had lived for a period amongst the fox-hunting squires, the gossiping attorneys and the rural deans of the English countryside; suppose, further, that when he decided to embark upon a domestic novel of contemporary life, he had chosen for his *milieu* the society of an English country town, what kind of a novel would have emerged? A partial answer may, perhaps, be sought in *St. Ronan's Well*, a book which was unfavourably received by many English critics, notably by Hazlitt, who declared that Scott must not come down from his fastnesses to the littleness and the frippery of modern civilisation. Hazlitt, of course, is too sweeping. Intoxicated by the pageantry of Scott's romantic narratives, he was incapable of an impartial approach to this experiment in domestic fiction. Certainly *St. Ronan's Well* is very far from being a failure. Meg Dods, the landlady of the Cleikum, is in the true Scott tradition; Cargill and Touchwood are attractive eccentrics; Bindloose, the country lawyer and Mrs. Blower, the sea-captain's widow, are entirely convincing. But Scott was too restlessly creative to concentrate his observation or his energy upon a microcosm. The petty jealousies, quarrels and intrigues of a health resort could not satisfy him; for his main plot he must have some of the elements of melodrama—a mock marriage, a fantastic will, pistol duels, death-bed confessions, and a heroine who meets with Ophelia's fate. No one, not even Mr. Forster, can complain of an idiotic marriage at the end of the book. Scott himself, who was forced to alter a passage in the story to satisfy his publisher's squeamishness, was not greatly pleased with his adventure into a new field: " I am too much out of the way," he wrote, " to see and remark the ridiculous in society," and he criticised the story as contorted and unnatural. Balzac, on the other hand, regarded it as a masterpiece.

For a glimpse of Scott's power to give what he called an imitation of the shifting manners of his own time, it might perhaps be better to turn to certain passages in his other novels—the opening chapters, for example, of *Redgauntlet*, or those chapters in *Guy Mannering* in which Pleydell is first introduced. There the professional and social life of Edinburgh lawyers is revealed in all its comedy and conviviality. Scott was very much in the way of that kind of life, and it is legitimate to conjecture what kind of a novel might have been built upon it. But speculations of such a kind are indeed of flimsy texture and may well lead to the lame conclusion that if Scott had been a different man he would have written a different kind of book.

Whether the Waverley Novels have been over-praised or whether they have been unfairly criticised; whether in the future they are destined to suffer neglect or whether some great revival will occur, there yet remains one work of Scott that will triumphantly defy every revolution of critical taste—his *Journal*. For in that record of his last seven years there is a revelation of the man, and of the man in the saddest period of his life. Trollope's *Autobiography* describes the poverty and struggle of his early years but, on the whole, it is a story of success. The greatness of Scott's *Journal* lies in the fact that it is a record of the years of failure and the record is free alike from false pride and from false modesty. The simple courage with which Scott faced his troubles has become almost proverbial; for it was " 2 o'clock in the morning " courage, and when vitality seemed lowest, Scott's spirit rose to its height:

> I might save my library, etc., by assistance of friends, and bid my creditors defiance. But for this I would, in a court of honour, deserve to lose my spurs. No, if they permit me, I will be their vassal for life. . . .

Perhaps it is the humanity, even more than the heroism, of the *Journal* that evokes affection. Here, for instance, is Scott's comment on his meeting with Tom Moore:

> We are both good-humoured fellows, who rather seek to enjoy what is going forward than to maintain our dignity as lions; and we have both seen the world too widely and too well not to contemn in our souls the imaginary consequences of literary people.

And all the time, with pardonable lapses (*peccavi, peccavi, dies quidem sine linea*) he remembered the biddings and the chidings of Madam Duty, accepting " patience and proof-sheets " as his daily lot. Sometimes his equanimity would temporarily fail him: " Devil take the necessity which makes me drudge like a very hack of Grub Street," and when his friend Huxley took his own life, Scott sadly reflected :

> My system, which is of the stoic school . . . is the only philosophy I know or can practise, but it cannot always keep the helm.

But two days later he wrote : " I am now once more at my oar and I will row hard."   And if ever he was tempted to grow sentimental, he quickly recalled Byron's remark to Moore : " Damn it, Tom, don't be poetical."

These are but fragments, *disjecta membra* of a body of reflections which are stamped with the impress of a stark, yet humorous, sincerity. Whatever may be the ultimate fate of the novels, the *Journal* remains as the imperishable document of a man who faced things as they were and greeted misfortune, as he had greeted prosperity, with a cheer. Infused with a gaiety and with a nobility which Time itself cannot antiquate, it is Scott's Testament of Duty.

INDEX

Abbot, The, 48
Abbotsford, 57, 58, 59, 61, 65, 144
Abercorn, Anne Jane Gore, Marchioness of, 60
Addison, Joseph, 92
Adolphus, John Leycester, 4-6, 7, 8, 9, 10, 21, 27, 30, 50, 56, 63
Æschylus, 21
Ainsworth, William Harrison, 36
"Albania," 20
Anne of Geierstein, 88
Antiquary, The, 13, 49, 50, 69, 76-77, 77, 95, 150-153, 154
Aristotle, 45
Arnold, Thomas, 105
Aubrey, John, 92
Austen, Jane, 33, 56, 84; Scott's review of *Emma*, 128, 129
Autobiography, quoted, 36, 38, 111-112, 113, 115

Bagehot, Walter, 6-7, 8, 9, 82-83, 88
Baillie, Joanna, 105, 117
Ballantyne, James, 8, 50, 122, 123, 132, 138
Balzac, Honoré de, 40, 63, 71, 163
Belsches, Williamina, Lady Forbes, 11, 60-64, 66
Bennett, Arnold, 41
Beresford, James, Scott's review of his *Miseries of Human Life*, 161
Blake, William, 16
Bride of Lammermoor, The, 30, 49, 63, 66, 67, 70, 74, 99-100
Brontë, Emily, 56
Browning, Robert, 16
Buchan, John, Lord Tweedsmuir. *See* Tweedsmuir
Bürger, Gottfried August, 118
Burke, Edmund, 9
Burney, Frances, Mme d'Arblay, 32, 36

Burns, Robert, 13, 16, 50, 115, 122-123
Butterfield, Herbert, 113-114
Byron, George Gordon Noel
Byron, Lord, 16, 30, 125, 165

Cadell, Robert, 147
Carlyle, Thomas, 42-43, 44, 146-147
Carpenter, Margaret Charlotte, Lady Scott. *See* Scott
Cervantes Saavedra, Miguel de, 50, 51
Chaucer, Geoffrey, 39, 48, 51, 72, 101, 102
Chesterton, G. K., 41
Chronicles of the Canongate, 84
"Clyde, The," 20
Cockburn, Henry Thomas, Lord Cockburn, vii, 7
Coleridge, Samuel Taylor, 16, 119, 122, 145-146
Collingwood, R. G., 44-45
Corelli, Marie, 34
Corneille, Pierre, 38, 39
Count Robert of Paris, 48, 49, 88
Cowper, William, 20
Crabbe, George, 6, 22, 23-24, 25-26, 124
Culloden Papers, quoted, 106-107

Dante Alighieri, 48
Defoe, Daniel, 96
Dickens, Charles, 6, 40, 57, 66, 73, 75, 84, 94
Doom of Devorgoil, quoted, 121-122
Dostoevsky, Fyodor Mikhailovitch, 75-76
Dryden, John, 4, 123

Edgeworth, Maria, 7, 38, 95, 95-96, 126

Edinburgh Review, The, 124, 136
Eliot, T. S., 11
Ellis, George, 16, 123
Erskine, William, Lord Kinnedder, 117, 124, 132
"Eve of Saint John, The," 118
Evelyn, John, 92

Fair Maid of Perth, The, 48
Feuchtwanger, Lion, 47
Fielding, Henry, 31, 34, 38, 40, 50, 73, 84, 127
Flaubert, Gustave, 41, 42, 44, 47
Forbes, Williamina Belsches, Lady. *See* Belsches
Forster, Edward Morgan, 69, 75, 148-152, 162
Fortunes of Nigel, The, 49, 50, 64, 71-72, 72, 74, 141-142
France, Anatole, 47
Froude, James Anthony, 105

Gibbon, Edward, 81
Godwin, William, 35
Goethe, Johann Wolfgang von, 103
Gordon, George Huntly, 117
Gray, Thomas, 115-116, 125
"Gray Brother, The," 118
Grierson, Sir H. J. C., 55, 154
Guizot, François-Pierre-Guillaume, 43
Guy Mannering, 13, 49, 50, 51, 77-78, 93-94, 98, 99, 138, 145, 154, 163

Hardy, Thomas, 10, 51, 140
Hazlitt, William, 147, 162
Heart of Midlothian, The, 13, 49, 50, 51, 70, 75, 98, 156-158, 159, 161
Hogg, James, 35
Homer, 17, 25, 82, 113
Horatius Flaccus, Quintus, 113
Housman, Alfred Edward, 10, 121, 122
Hugo, Victor, 36, 40
Huizinga, Johan, 41, 45, 46
Huxley, Thomas, 165

Ibsen, Henrik, 51
Irving, Washington, 18
Ivanhoe, 14-15, 47, 48, 49, 86-87, 97, 142, 154

James, G. P. R., 36
Jeffrey, Francis, Lord Jeffrey, 124, 136
"Jock of Hazeldean," 13
Johnson, Samuel, 8, 31-32, 45-46, 46, 92, 99, 117, 123, 136
Journal, 10, 142, 163-165; quoted, 4, 9, 24, 60, 116
Joyce, James, 59, 62

Keats, John, 21, 25, 57
Kenilworth, 49, 50
Kingston, W. H., 36

Lacaid, Dennis, 46-47
Lady of the Lake, The, 17, 18, 37, 124; quoted, 12, 29, 82-83
Lang, Andrew, 160
Larreta, Enrique, 42, 47
Lay of the Last Minstrel, The, vii, viii, 12, 16, 17, 119-120; quoted, 23, 27-28, 28-29
Legend of Montrose, A, 49
Lewis, Matthew Gregory, 11, 35, 37
Lives of the Novelists, 128
Lockhart, John Gibson, 8, 49, 133, 138, 139, 146, 154
Lord of the Isles, The, 17, 138

Macaulay, Thomas Babington Macaulay, Lord, 43, 93, 94, 105
Macaulay, Zachary, 145
Mackenzie, Henry, Bishop of Nottingham, 147
Mackenzie, Henry, "Man of Feeling," 36
Marmion, 17, 25, 28, 87, 123-124; quoted, 12, 18-20, 22, 24, 26, 83
Meredith, George, 40
Michelet, Jules, 43
Mill, John Stuart, 112
Milton, John, 17, 21, 112

INDEX

Minstrelsy of the Scottish Border, 118, 125
Monastery, The, viii, 48, 89-91, 97
Moore, Thomas, 30, 164, 165
Morris, William, 17
Morritt, J. B. S., 120, 132
Motley, John Lothrop, 43

Napoleon I, Emperor of the French, 103-105

Old Mortality, 49, 50, 72, 73, 93, 96
Ossian, 20

Pearsall Smith, Logan. *See* Smith
Percy, Thomas, Bishop of Dromore, 113, 118
Peveril of the Peak, 91
Poe, Edgar Allan, 11
Pope, Alexander, 92, 112, 113
Porter, Jane, 35
Pottle, Frederick Albert, 157
Prescott, William Hickling, 43
"Proud Maisie," 14, 66, 121
Proust, Marcel, 41
Purdie, Tom, 106

Quarterly Review, 137, 148
Quentin Durward, 15, 50, 84, 154

Racine, Jean, 38, 39
Radcliffe, Anne, 34, 35, 37, 39, 88, 94; Scott's essay on, quoted, 36
Raleigh, Sir Walter, 129
Redgauntlet, 47, 49, 66, 67-68, 84, 98, 102, 154, 163
Reeve, Clara, 96
Religious discourses, 117
Richardson, Samuel, 31, 34, 126
Rickert, Heinrich, 43
Rob Roy, 49, 74, 77, 84, 85-86, 95, 96, 102
Robertson, William, 99
Robinson, Henry Crabb, 145
Rokeby, 12-13
Ruskin, John, 24, 25, 26, 28, 84

Sainte-Beuve, Charles-Augustin de, 103

St. Ronan's Well, 50, 84, 162-163
Saintsbury, George Edward Bateman, 95
Schiller, Friedrich von, 34, 35
Scott, Margaret Charlotte Carpenter, Lady, 60
Seccombe, Thomas, 154
Shakespeare, William, 14, 16, 21, 38, 39, 51, 62, 101, 102
Shelley, Percy Bysshe, 16, 26, 35
Smith, Catharine, 35
Smith, Logan Pearsall, 91
Smith, Sydney, 7
Smollett, Tobias, 31, 38, 40, 50
Southey, Robert, 120
Spenser, Edmund, 113
Sterne, Laurence, 56, 75, 84
Stevenson, Robert Louis, 42
Stoddart, Sir John, 119
Strutt, Joseph, his *Queenhoo-Hall*, 37, 41, 126, 127
Swift, Jonathan, 9

Taine, Hippolyte, 118
Tennyson, Alfred Tennyson, Lord, 25, 26, 28
Thackeray, William Makepeace, 41, 56, 57, 73, 74, 84
Thierry, Augustin, 87
Thomas the Rhymer, 37
Thomson, James, 20
Tolstoy, Count Leo, 63
Trollope, Anthony, 32, 95, 140-144, 154-160, 164
Trollope, Mrs. Frances, 36
Tweedsmuir, John Buchan, 1st Baron, 57, 62, 129, 154
"Two Drovers, The," 97, 99

"Violet, The," 11
Virgilius Maro, Publius, 17, 113
Voltaire, François-Marie-Arouet de, 99

Walpole, Horace, 32, 33, 37, 88, 125
Waverley, 13, 37, 48, 49, 50, 96, 125-138, 140, 145

Wellington, Arthur Wellesley, Duke of, 105
Whitman, Walt, 11
Wilson, John, "Christopher North," 148
Windelband, Wilhelm, 43

Woodstock, 15, 67, 91
Woolf, Virginia, 152-153, 154
Wordsworth, William, 21, 26, 56, 57, 66, 104, 105

Yeats, William Butler, 16

THE END